Discovering
the Pearl *of*
Great Price
The Parables of Jesus

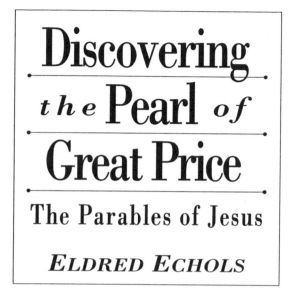

Discovering
the Pearl *of*
Great Price

The Parables of Jesus

ELDRED ECHOLS

— *A* —

FAITH*FOCUS*

Book

Sweet Publishing
Fort Worth, Texas

Discovering the Pearl of Great Price
The Parables of Jesus

Copyright © 1992 by Sweet Publishing,
Fort Worth, TX 76137

Scripture quotations, unless otherwise noted, are from the Holy
Bible: New International Version. © 1973, 1978, 1984 by the
International Bible Society. Used by permission of Zondervan
Bible Publishers.

Cover: Blanchard Design

Library of Congress Catalog Number 92-60908

ISBN: 0-8344-0223-8

Printed in the U. S. A.
10 9 8 7 6 5 4 3 2

In loving memory
of my wife Jane,
who possessed a faith that
by far transcended mine.

Contents

Introduction   1

1 Discovering the Pearl of Great Price   5
   Discovery: Only Christ could pay
   the price.
   The Great Pearl —Matthew13:45, 46
   Hidden Treasure—Matthew 13:44

2 Removing My Heart Mask   17
   Discovery: There's joy in my true
   repentance.
   Prodigal Son—Luke 15:11-32
   Two Sons—Matthew 21:28-32

3 The Difficulty of Accepting God's Grace   31
   Discovery: Grace defies logic.
   Workers in the Vineyard—Matthew 20:1-16

4 Forgiving from the Heart   43
   Discovery: Forgiving others is essential
   to my forgiveness.
   Unmerciful Servant—Matthew 18:21-35

5 What Do You Expect from Prayer?   55
   Discovery: God always answers me quickly.
   Friend at Midnight—Luke 11:5-13
   Unrighteous Judge—Luke 18:1-8
   Pharisee and the Tax Collector—Luke 18:9-14

6 Is Money Your God?   71
   Discovery: I am called to make the most
   of what I have.
   Shrewd Manager—Luke16:1-13

vii

7 Loving the Unloveable   85
    Discovery: Loving others shows my
       love for God.
    Good Samaritan—Luke 10:25-37

8 Spiritual Gifts from God   99
    Discovery: God has a special purpose for me.
    The Talents—Matthew 25:14-30

9 Selfishness Leads to Hell   111
    Discovery: What I have is not mine to own.
    Rich Man and Lazarus—Luke 16:19-31

10 We Are a Sowing People   123
    Discovery: Even I can share my faith.
    The Soils—Matthew 13:3-9, 18-23
    The Wheat and Weeds—Matthew 13:24-30, 36-43
    The Growing Seed—Mark 4:26-29

11 Why Don't You Grow Up?   139
    Discovery: God turns my small
       beginnings into great endings.
    Mustard Seed and Yeast—Matthew 13:31-33

12 The Wisdom of Preparation   153
    Discovery: My saving faith is always
       growing.
    Ten Virgins—Matthew 25:1-13
    Watchful Servants—Mark 13:32-37

13 You Are Invited to the Banquet   167
    Discovery: I am clothed with Christ.
    Wedding Feast—Matthew 22:1-14

Introduction

The use of parables to teach cultural values pre-dates written history and is common to all races of mankind. Exact definitions of what constitutes a parable differ widely. Strictly speaking, any form of communication which illustrates a point by relating a parallel circumstance to the situation being addressed is a parable.

The word parable comes from the Greek *parabole* which signifies something which has been "laid alongside" something else. Some parables are simple proverbs: "Like a gold ring in a pig's snout is a beautiful woman who shows no discretion" (Proverbs 11:22). Others, like Aesop's fables, are charming stories that contain moral principles. The first recorded biblical parable is Jotham's allegory about the trees who sought a king to reign over them (Judges 9:7-15). Many of our traditional English nursery rhymes were, in fact, satirical parables about the reigning monarch. Ancient Romans scribbled parables on walls criticizing the excesses of some of the Caesars.

There are a number of reasons for using parables as tools for teaching or emphasizing a message. One of the principal reasons is that they use a less direct, less confrontational approach to a problem. In most primitive cultures there is a great reluctance to face unpleasant situations head on. Generally speaking, the less developed the society in terms of what Westerners like to call (often inaccurately) "civilization," the greater the emphasis on more polite, less abrasive forms of communication. Particularly, it is important not to rebuke a socially or politically superior person directly. A good example of this is the prophet Nathan's parable to David (2 Samuel 12:1-6).

A second reason is that the parable story is often a gripping tale that is not soon forgotten. So it serves as an easy reminder of the lesson it is intended to teach. It tends to hold the attention of the audience more readily than a factual sermon.

Jesus was the master teller of parables. He used them to teach his disciples truths which they were not yet able to understand, but which they would later recall and understand fully. He used them to teach hostile audiences that would have stopped their ears if he had spoken plainly. By the time he had finished the parable, his point had been made before they could shut him down.

Opinions differ on how many parables Jesus told, because opinions differ on what constitutes a parable. The number, by most criteria, would be between 30 and 40. Some are simply similitudes. Others are spell-binding narratives that play upon the emotions and find a permanent place in the hearts and memories of mankind, like the prodigal son (Luke 15).

These 13 lessons on the parables of Jesus attempt to relate these masterpieces of instruction to twenty-first century modes of thinking, and hopefully to restore some of the original color that may have been lost in translations.

Parable of the Great Pearl

Again, the kingdom of heaven is like a merchant looking for fine pearls. When he found one of great value, he went away and sold everything he had and bought it.

Matthew 13:45, 46

Parable of the Hidden Treasure

The kingdom of heaven is like treasure hidden in a field. When a man found it, he hid it again, and then in his joy went and sold all he had and bought that field.

Matthew 13:44

Chapter 1

Discovering
t h e Pearl *of*
Great Price

D r. Williamson had been slipping and sliding along the rain-soaked road that led through the back country of Tanzania. His work as a Canadian geologist often took him to deserted and difficult areas. Suddenly the Land Rover sunk up to its axles in the sticky mire and stopped short.

Discovery Point:

Only Christ could pay the price.

Pulling his shovel from the back of the vehicle, Dr. Williamson began the unpleasant task of digging his four-wheel drive out of the mud hole it had dug for itself. He had been at it for a long time when his shovel uncovered something strange. It was a pink-like stone of some sort. Being a geologist and naturally curious about rock formations, he picked it up and wiped away the mud. The more mud he removed, the more excited he became, but hardly believed what he was seeing. At last the stone was clean, and Dr. Williamson was overcome. He had found a diamond.

Now, any diamond at all would be a surprise in that situation. But Dr. Williamson had found the famous giant pink diamond of Tanzania. That muddy stone sparkles today in the royal scepter of Britain, and Dr. Williamson is world renowned for his find—accidental though it was.

Parable of the Great Pearl Matthew 13:45, 46

In the parable of the great pearl, Jesus tells of another man who made a great find. Jesus tells the parable in a few short words, but what a wealth of meaning they hold! He simply begins by saying that a merchant was looking for fine pearls.

Organic Origin

The pearl is unique among gemstones because of its organic origin; that is, it is a product of a living organism. Specifically, the fine quality pearls of the jewelry trade are obtained from several species of the pearl oyster, found in the Indo-Pacific Ocean. Since this mollusk thrives in tropical waters at an average depth of forty feet, a pearl is not a treasure a man will just happen to stumble onto while walking along the beach.

Pearls are not found like that. In biblical times they were obtained at great cost in human terms off the coast of Ceylon and in the Persian Gulf. Divers operating from small boats dived into the dangerous reefs carrying a large stone attached to a rope to pull them down to the depths of the oyster beds. They risked attacks from sharks, moray eels, and devil fish. Some were able to stay submerged for up to five minutes gathering the shellfish. Yet, an average of only one oyster in a thousand contained a pearl. The divers were old men at thirty and generally did not survive the age of forty. Rarely, a diver brought up a gem of priceless quality, but stones weighing up to two hundred and fifty carats have been found. The former Maharajah of Hyderabad (India) was reputed to keep a bag of pearls beneath his throne, some as large as pigeon eggs. But no pearls were found in ancient times except at the risk of a man's life.

Perfect Pearls

A second extraordinary characteristic of the pearl is that it is the only gem that cannot be improved by man. All other jewels must be cut and polished by skilled craftsmen to have value as gemstones. Raw diamonds, for example, look like rather unattractive lumps of glass until they are faceted and polished. But the natural iridescence of a pearl is perfect

---

Any attempts on the part of human creatures to meddle with or try to improve the great Creator's kingdom defaces it and robs it of its perfection.

---

when it is found and cannot be improved by cutting and polishing. One cut from a human hand and the pearl is worthless.

This makes the pearl a particularly appropriate symbol for the kingdom of God. For the kingdom is a divine institution, designed by the mind of a perfect God from times eternal. Any attempts on the part of human creatures to meddle with or try to improve the great Creator's kingdom defaces it and robs it of its perfection.

The great men of the Bible were "pearl seekers." Hebrews chapter eleven lists some leading men of faith who were looking for something of greater value than were most people of their times. Notable among them were the three grand Hebrew fathers Abraham, Isaac, and Jacob. They lived as aliens in a country far from their homeland, nomads in tents because they sought a pearl of great value. They were "looking forward to the city with foundations, whose architect and builder is God" (verse 10). Others, like the ancient pearl divers of the Persian Gulf, gave up their lives in the search: "They were stoned; they were sawed in two; they were put to death by the sword" (verse 37).

The Kingdom Defined

The kingdom of God exists in a spiritual dimension that always transcends the physical universe. It exists wherever God reigns in the hearts of his subjects. In a very limited sense, it was present in the divinely ruled government of covenant Israel. God was their king, and they were his subjects. His law governed every aspect of their lives. We know from the New Testament that the kingdom is God's ruling or reigning activity in the lives of people.

In a much fuller sense, the church is a realized phase of the kingdom. That kingdom could not exist until Christ's crucifixion broke down the barrier of sin that separated people from God, and the human spirit could have communion again with him. The final phase of the kingdom will be reached only when the mortal bodies of the saints have been redeemed to immortality (Romans 8:23). In every age of the kingdom, God is found by those who seek him:

In the Mosaic Age—Deuteronomy 4:29;
Isaiah 55:6, 7; Jeremiah 29:13;

In the Age of Christ's Church—
Matthew 6:33; 7:7, 8;

In the Age of the Heavenly Kingdom—
Acts 14:22; Romans 2:6, 7; Colossians
3:1-4.

But the kingdom must be sought first; that is, it
must be the first priority of the seeker and more
important to him than earthly values (Matthew
6:33). The pearl cannot be found by the casual
wayfarer. God rewards only those who through faith
earnestly seek him (Hebrews 11:6).

The Ultimate Merchant

The ultimate merchant seeking a flawless pearl
was the perfect Son of God himself. He "emptied
himself"—he gave up his divinity and all the glories
of heaven to purchase the great pearl, his kingdom,
with his own priceless life. He came "to seek and to
save what was lost" (Luke 19:10). As an analogy, a
parable can only capture limited aspects of the
reality it is illustrating. In shopping for pearls a
merchant would certainly not voluntarily give his
life for one gem, however rare it might be. So, no
imaginative comparison can convey more than a
pale shadow of the enormous price God paid to
redeem his people. The analogy also breaks down in
the inherent value of the pearl between the time the
merchant found it and the time he bought it. The
pearl was as perfect as it could ever be before it was
found. The price paid for it only confirmed its great
value.

The kingdom, on the other hand, is made up of
people who "were dead in [their] transgressions and

sins . . . and followed the ways of this world and of
the ruler of the kingdom of the air, the spirit who is
now at work in those who are disobedient"
(Ephesians 2:1, 2). The allegory of Hosea's purchase
of his wayward wife well illustrates the point: she
was a disgraced and destitute slave when Hosea
found her. Yet, he sold even his store of food in order
to buy her back. She was lovely only to Hosea (Hosea
1–3). In just this way God loved us when we were
unlovable. "But God demonstrates his own love for
us in this: While we were still sinners, Christ died
for us" (Romans 5:8).

> ## *Salvation is a gift of God! We can't buy it or earn it because the price is too high.*

It's important to see that only the priceless Son of
God was valuable enough to exchange for the priceless pearl the kingdom of God. Only his blood could
satisfy the demanded price of the great pearl. Then,
when Christ owned the precious pearl of salvation,
he graciously shared it with his faithful followers
and earthly companions—us.

So then, we are saved by his grace through our
faithful belief and obedience to him. Salvation is a
gift of God! We can't buy it or earn it because the
price is too high. We can only accept it as an incredible gift of love from a dying Friend and continue to
do good things out of our overwhelming gratitude to
him. That gratitude leads us to strive to be more and
more like Christ—pearl seekers, willing to give up
everything in this life for the pearl of great price—
God's kingdom.

Parable of the Hidden Treasure Matthew 13:44

A companion parable to the great pearl is the parable of the hidden treasure. In this story a man finds a treasure hidden in a field, hides it again, then excitedly goes and sells everything he has to buy the field. Jesus introduces the allegory by saying the treasure represents his kingdom. Presumably, the field is the world at large. The man, like the merchant in the previous story, might represent more than one counterpart. In a general way, he might represent anyone who is truly seeking the kingdom of God. The immediate and primary application is obviously Christ himself.

Was Jesus Unethical?

This parable has appeared to many to condone questionable, if not downright unethical, behavior. They might say that if something valuable is buried in a piece of ground, doesn't it belong by first right to the owner of the land, and the finder must report it either to the owner or to the proper authorities? Actually, finder's rights differ from country to country. They generally provide for the finder and owner to share in the treasure, but the finder usually cannot simply take the treasure.

However, these objectives do not apply to the elements of this parable. In the first place, the "landowner" is a usurper, Satan. He has asserted "squatter's rights," having forcefully taken the property (the world) from its true owner by deceit. Jesus calls the devil "the prince of this world" (John 12:31; 14:30), but he is simply making a statement of practical fact, not acknowledging Satan's right to ownership. Satan is, after all, only the prince; Christ is the King—the true owner of the world.

The Hidden Secret

The treasure is not visible to anyone except the finder. Why? Because it has never been exposed to public view. The treasure is the kingdom in embryo. It's God's people as they existed in his mind from eternity, but he has waited to reveal until the fullness of time has come. God has all knowledge to see things to come as though they already were (1 Corinthians 1:28). He saw the kingdom of Christ our Lord in the secret plan he had for the salvation

---

Only His blood could satisfy the demanded price of the great pearl.

---

of mankind. Although not even in existence, God's plan was potentially more powerful than all of Satan's worldly systems. As Paul declared in Ephesians 1:3, 4, God foresaw Christ as head over his chosen people, but it was a mystery not to be divulged until the gospel age. It was a wisdom that had to be kept hidden from the usurper (Satan) who wrongfully controlled the field, or he would destroy the treasure (salvation) (1 Corinthians 2:6-10). It would only work if the devil didn't find it out. For everything depended upon God in the flesh (in the form of his Son) being nailed to a cross—something Satan would never have done if he had realized that in shedding Jesus' blood he was forging his own chain of defeat.

The Surprise Victory

It was a perfect plan, but the price was stupendously high. Satan never guessed God would pay it.

It depended upon Christ, the eternal Word, taking
on humanity and coming to repossess the field
(kingdom) by conquering the false king. At the close
of his ministry, when Jesus stood in the shadow of
the cross, he exclaimed to his disciples, "Take heart!
I have overcome the world" (John 16:33). He had
bought the field with his life, and the kingdom
treasure was his! Like the pearl of great price,
Christ alone could find and buy the hidden treasure
in the field. Two reasons:

- He was the only one who had "eyes" to
  see the hidden treasure (salvation). No
  one else, not even Satan, had the divine
  insight necessary to see it. God had
  hidden the treasure from everyone else.

- He was the only one who could pay the
  price for the field—his blood.

In a lesser but very real sense, every seeker of the
kingdom must overcome the world if he is to possess
the treasure of the kingdom. Jesus' apostles left
everything they owned (Matthew 19:27); Paul lost
all things for Christ's sake (Philippians 3:8); and we
must all overcome the power of this world if we
would reign with Christ on his heavenly throne
(Revelation 3:21). It means we must take up our
cross (Matthew 10:38) and be crucified to the world
(Galatians 5:24). We must be willing to "pay the
price." We must be willing to give up everything to
become a joint owner of the land with full rights to
the treasure—salvation in the kingdom of God.

Pearl of Wisdom:

*Salvation, which is
the pearl of great price
and the treasure in the
field, could only be
purchased by Christ.
Then, by his grace, he
gave this salvation as
his gift to us who focus
our faith on him.*

Focusing Your Faith

1. In your view, what is the main point of this chapter?

2. Why is it tempting to all humans to fashion salvation to our own specifications instead of accepting it as God designed it?

3. How does God reign actively in your life as a citizen of his kingdom? In your work? With your family? In social settings?

4. What if God had decided *not* to pay the price for the kingdom? What feelings do you experience when you think of that?

5. What are some of the ways you presently see yourself expressing your personal gratitude to God for the salvation you have because of his grace?

6. Imagine that Jesus, who paid his life for the kingdom, spoke to you face to face. What would he say to you personally? What would you say to him?

7. What could the kingdom of God on earth accomplish if Christians truly allowed God to rule and reign in their lives? And what can you accomplish personally?

Parable of the Prodigal Son

Jesus continued: "There was a man who had two sons. The younger one said to his father, 'Father, give me my share of the estate.' So he divided his property between them.

"Not long after that, the younger son got together all he had, set off for a distant country and there squandered his wealth in wild living. After he had spent everything, there was a severe famine in that whole country, and he began to be in need. So he went and hired himself out to a citizen of that country, who sent him to his fields to feed pigs. He longed to fill his stomach with the pods that the pigs were eating, but no one gave him anything. "When he came to his senses, he said, 'How many of my father's hired men have food to spare, and here I am starving to death! I will set out and go back to my father and say to him: Father, I have sinned against heaven and against you. I am no longer worthy to be called your son; make me like one of your hired men.' So he got up and went to his father.

"But while he was still a long way off, his father saw him and was filled with compassion for him; he ran to his son, threw his arms around him and kissed him.

"The son said to him, 'Father, I have sinned against heaven and against you. I am no longer worthy to be called your son.'

"But the father said to his servants, 'Quick! Bring the best robe and put it on him. Put a ring on his finger and sandals on his feet. Bring the fattened calf and kill it. Let's have a feast and celebrate. For this son of mine was dead and is alive again; he was lost and is found.' So they began to celebrate.

"Meanwhile, the older son was in the field. When he came near the house, he heard music and dancing. So he called one of the servants and asked him what was going on. 'Your brother has come,' he replied, 'and your father has killed the fattened calf because he has him back safe and sound.'

"The older brother became angry and refused to go in. So his father went out and pleaded with him. But he answered his father, 'Look! All these years I've been slaving for you and never disobeyed your orders. Yet you never gave me even a young goat so I could celebrate with my friends. But when this son of yours who has squandered your property with prostitutes comes home, you kill the fattened calf for him!'

" 'My son,' the father said, 'you are always with me, and everything I have is yours. But we had to celebrate and be glad, because this brother of yours was dead and is alive again; he was lost and is found.' "

Luke 15:11-32

Chapter 2

Removing
My
Heart Mask

"It's not you; it's me. I've got to go find out who I am and why I'm here." That was the note found in the bedroom of a fourteen-year-old boy named Damon in a Southern California town in 1974. He didn't come home.

Discovery Point:

There's joy in my true repentance.

From that moment on, turmoil, family trauma, pain, guilt, and resentment plagued this average Christian family. The mom, dad, brother, and sister went to church as usual, but everything seemed different. There was always an empty place at the table and in the car.

For ten long years, the parents watched and waited, but there was not a trace, not a word, not a reason for their son's running away. The truth is, he was caught up in the occult. He was treading the satanic path to destruction, even though he didn't even realize it himself.

On Christmas day of 1984 the family heard a knock on the door. Standing on the porch was their long-lost, now-grown son Damon with his wife and two children.

It was the first contact of any type in over ten years. Without hesitation the parents reached out in love and drew in their son and his family. Their season of pain and anguish dissolved into the joy of celebration. On Christmas day their son was born again.

Damon's sister resented his unexpected return and her parents' ready acceptance of him back into their good graces after all the pain and trauma he had caused the family through the years. She stalked out of the room to show her disapproval. Then for years the parents had to work to win her back too.

This true, present-day story relives Jesus' parable in Luke 15 about the prodigal younger son and his prodigal older brother.

Parable of the Prodigal Son Luke 15:11-32

The poignantly beautiful story we have traditionally called the "parable of the prodigal son" is actually much more than that. It reflects the needs of Jesus' audience. On one side were the sinners and tax collectors who had been "written off" by the Jewish religious elite. These "low lifes" were considered beyond the limits of God's forgiveness, but they longed desperately for some word of hope. On the other side were the Pharisees and teachers of the law who were smug in their self-righteousness and harshly judged anyone who disagreed with their rigid view of the Scriptures.

Turning Away

Jesus tells a story about the two sons of a farmer. The younger son was restless and bored with his life. So, he decided to leave his father's house and see what the world had to offer an adventurous youth with money in his pocket. He soon found that the world had a great deal to offer in short-term pleasures and excitement to a free spender with a flexible conscience.

Jesus does not dwell on what must have been a painful parting of the son from the father. Knowing the nature of his younger son and the way of the world with inexperienced youths, the father must surely have sternly warned, pleaded, and beseeched the younger man with many tears. We know only the bare essentials. The boy demanded the share of the inheritance that would be due him at his father's death. The father gave in to his demand, and the young man wasted no time in setting out on his great adventure.

> *He had turned away from his father, and in doing so had turned from a prince to a pig.*

After turning his assets into currency, the younger son turned his back on his home and was soon living it up in the fleshpots of the Middle East. The morals training of his childhood was abandoned like a worn-out coat as he plunged into the dingy world of gambling dives, wine, women and song. As always, the world exacted a heavy price for his fleeting pleasures, and the day eventually came when the young man's last shekel was handed over.

Then the greedy, callous world threw him out into
the streets of a foreign land. There was no friend to
give him so much as a bread crust. He was suddenly
just one of the homeless street people, sleeping in
doorways and digging through the refuse of his
wealthy former "friends" for a morsel of food for
survival, like the desperate homeless we pass on our
city streets today.

How many requests for employment were turned
down we'll never know, but the job he finally got was
feeding pigs for a Gentile farmer—the ultimate
humiliation for a rich Jew. As he pulled carob beans
from the trees and fed them to the squealing hogs, he
was so famished that he began chewing the pods
himself.

He had turned away from his father, and in doing
so had turned from a prince to a pig.

Turning Around

Finally, from the smelly muck of the pigsty, he
took stock of himself and was repulsed by what he
saw. His disturbed thoughts slowly turned toward
home, and nostalgia racked his soul. The text says,
"He came to his senses." The mad course of a
libertine's life was ended, and he was left homeless
and broken. Then for the first time since he had set
out from home, he was open to help.

Only when all of his resources were exhausted and
he had no other way to go did he turn his heart
toward the loving home where he had the only true
friend in all the world—his father. Then it dawned on
him that he no longer had a legitimate claim as a son
upon his father. What could he do? He was unworthy
of his father's love. It was then he resolved to go
back and throw himself upon his parent's mercy,
confess his sin, and plead to become only a hired
servant. Humble and repentant, he went.

Turning Out Right

The old father saw his son long before he got to the house. How many times must the father have stood in the fading twilight looking with longing down that road his son had taken when he left, hoping above hope to see a familiar silhouette against the sky only to turn away disappointed. Then, at long last, he saw it—that familiar gait and form in the weary figure approaching. With surpassing joy the old man threw open the front door and ran to meet his beloved child, sweeping him into his arms and crying with the incredible joy of relief and love.

The young man made a desperate attempt to put things back into perspective and blurted out his rehearsed confession, but the father wasn't listening. He was too busy telling the servants to prepare a celebration in honor of his son's return. And what a party it was!

Turning Aside

Not everyone living on that farm was in a festive mood that day. The elder brother had finished his work in the field and was coming toward the house. Incredibly, he heard the sounds of celebration coming from the farm house—a house that had known little joy for a long time. He asked one of the hired hands what was going on, and his worst nightmare was confirmed. The rogue had returned, and his father was treating him as a hero. It was a celebration that insulted all propriety; so, the elder brother indignantly refused to go in.

The father went out and pleaded with him to come in and be a part of the joy. But the elder son had a few things to get off his chest, and the words poured out in a bitter torrent: "All these years I've worked

like a dog, and what did I get for my trouble? You
never even barbecued a goat for me to have a little
party with my friends.But when this rascal you call
'son,' who has blown your money on prostitutes,
comes slinking back, you have quite outdone yourself
by butchering our corn-fed steer!"

We learn that repentance is for our benefit, not God's.

The father was deeply pained and exclaimed,
"Why son, this whole farm is yours. Your place is not
threatened. But what you don't seem to realize is
that we have received your brother back home, when
we had given him up for dead. A lost boy has been
found, and we have more than enough reason to
celebrate." The self-righteous older brother refused
his father's plea. Isn't it ironic that the long-time
"faithful" older son is now on the outside while the
renegade-but-repentant younger son ends up inside
with the father.

As Jesus finished his wonderful story, we can
imagine the mixed reaction it caused in his audience. The outcasts who were listening—the moral
bankrupts of Jewish society, who were used to
rejection by the Jewish elite—heard the incredible
message of hope that God had never given up on
them. They would be welcome to come home again!
They rejoiced and turned to God.

The proud, self-righteous Pharisees sniffed in
disdain, but not in surprise. This self-appointed
Preacher from Galilee, who had not so much as
attended a rabbinical school, had aligned himself
with the riffraff of the community. It was an outrage. For, of course, they knew that the younger
brother represented the harlots, drunkards, thieves,

and tax collectors who were being offered the forgiveness of a gracious God. The superior elder brother represented the arrogant Pharisees and teachers of the law. They spurned the kingdom because they didn't want a share in it if undesirables were going to be allowed in also. Jesus warned them, "I tell you the truth, the tax collectors and the prostitutes are entering the kingdom of God ahead of you" (Matthew 21:31). He charged them with "You shut the kingdom of heaven in men's faces. You yourselves do not enter, nor will you let those enter who are trying to" (Matthew 23:14).

There was soon to be a much wider application of the parable when the gospel was preached to the Gentiles. Jews, for the most part, rejected a message of salvation that offered grace to the hated Romans and Greeks. They felt that 1500 years of law keeping entitled them to special privileges (which they had a right to anyhow as Abraham's children) and that it was a preposterous perversion of justice to allow uncircumcised Johnny-come-lately Gentiles an equal share of God's grace. Like the elder brother of Jesus' parable, the Jews most often chose not to come inside rather than accept as brethren people they had been brought up to call "dogs in the marketplace."

Our Turn

We, too, may exclude ourselves from the kingdom if we do not welcome into our hearts and fellowship people who, for whatever reason, are different from ourselves. When the outcasts and street people— either physically, socially, or emotionally—come back home to God, we should represent the Father by throwing open the church door and running out to meet them. We need to throw the party, celebrate, sing and cry in joyful reception on his behalf.

God has given us this parable to show his reaction to our repentance. Just look at the father's response to the returning son—joyful tears, thanksgiving, embraces, music, party! And we learn that repentance is for *our* benefit, not God's. It enables us to see him in his loving, accepting role—to experience the joy of being loved by him for just who we are, a son or daughter.

Every person "sins and falls short of the glory of God." That means every person must repent and turn back to God by changing his heart and life. We cannot avoid our need to repent by "doing good deeds" or through ministry or through church attendance, because even the most active Christian is imperfect and needs God's accepting forgiveness. This parable shows that every person is capable of repenting, even the most rebellious and flamboyant sinner among us. God welcomes home *every* sinner who repents and returns to him.

Parable of the Two Sons Matthew 21:28-32

Similar to the prodigal son parable is Jesus' story about another farmer and his two sons. Jesus directed this story at the chief priests and elders of the Jews. This elite group felt threatened by Jesus' teaching because they made great pretense of being righteous. They paid meticulous attention to outward rites and ceremonies, but they cared little for the problems of their people. To adapt Jesus' quote, they "cleaned the outside of the cup and dish, but inside they were full of greed and self-indulgence" (Matthew 23:25). Thousands of the common people had repented at the preaching of John the Baptizer, but the religious leaders dismissed the ministry of John by saying that he had a demon (Luke 7:33).

Parable of the Two Sons

"What do you think? There was a man who had two sons. He went to the first and said, 'Son, go and work today in the vineyard.'

" 'I will not,' he answered, but later he changed his mind and went.

"Then his father went to the other son and said the same thing. He answered, 'I will, sir,' but he did not go.

"Which of the two did what his father wanted?"

"The first," they answered.

Jesus said to them, "I tell you the truth, the tax collectors and the prostitutes are entering the kingdom of God ahead of you. For John came to you to show you the way of righteousness, and you did not believe him, but the tax collectors and the prostitutes did. And even after you saw this, you did not repent and believe him."

Matthew 21:28-32

Taking Turns

Jesus said a farmer had two sons. He told one son to go work in the vineyard, but the son replied that he would not go. Later, after thinking about his refusal, he decided he was taking the wrong course. So he repented of his rebelliousness and went to work in the vineyard. The father also went to his other son and gave him the same instruction he had given the first. The boy readily agreed to go, but he never went.

Jesus then asked his audience to tell him which son had obeyed the father. They were forced to reply that it was the first one. Then Jesus drove home the point of his story.

Obedience to God is much more than lip service.

The religious establishment—the priests, rabbis, scribes, and the Pharisees posed as the religious examples of the community in obedience to God's will. They were pious in their speech and demeanor but were really unrepentant frauds and hypocrites, eager to tell others what to do but unwilling to "lift one finger" themselves (Luke 11:46). They were represented by the second son in Jesus' story.

The tax collectors and prostitutes, on the other hand, were openly unfaithful to God. They pursued a lifestyle that was completely rebellious toward God. But when John came preaching about repentance and showed them the way back to God, they eagerly took it. "The tax collectors and the prostitutes are entering the kingdom of God ahead of you," Jesus said to the Pharisees (Matthew 21:31). But their ears were deaf to his warning. They felt no need for repentance. They had woven hypocrisy into their religious lives to such a degree that the pretense had become reality to them.

God holds no grudges.

From this lesson we learn that obedience to God is much more than lip service. "Let's pretend" is a game played in religion in every age. God spoke through Isaiah to Israel: "These people come near to me with their mouth and honor me with their lips, but their hearts are far from me. Their worship of me is made up only of rules taught by men" (Isaiah 29:13). Paul warned Timothy that people who love themselves rather than God have a form of godliness but deny its power (2 Timothy 3:5).

Secondly, God holds no grudges. However wicked a person has once been, there is no residue of evil when he repents and returns to God. God no longer sees what he was but what he *wants* to be. "Though your sins are like scarlet, they shall be as white as snow; though they are red as crimson, they shall be like wool" (Isaiah 1:18).

It is not true that you can't go home again. There is always one home where the door is open as long as this age shall last. And the Father is watching with longing to see your familiar gait as you humbly and penitently come back home.

Pearl of Wisdom:

We can find great joy in true repentance. Historically, we have refused to accept the benefits of repentance because it's difficult for us to see beyond our sin, like the prodigal son in the far country. But the benefits are there, if we just reach out through repentance and take them.

Focusing Your Faith

1. What was the most important point of this chapter to you personally?

2. Do you feel the father in this parable was really fair to the older brother who had worked so hard for him all those years? Why?

3. Imagine that your own child ran away from home and was gone for several months. What would you want your child to hear you say at your reunion? (After you decide, why not say it to your child today?)

4. Why do you think the younger son in this parable really left home?

5. If this parable were a play and you an actor/actress, which part do you see yourself playing most naturally? Why?

6. At the end of this parable, the family is still dysfunctional. If no attitudes change, what do you see this family becoming as time goes on? If the older son's attitude changes in a positive way, what could happen?

7. How does this lesson from Jesus specifically apply to your own family today and in the future?

Parable of the Workers in the Vineyard

"For the kingdom of heaven is like a landowner who went out early in the morning to hire men to work in his vineyard. He agreed to pay them a denarius for the day and sent them into his vineyard.

"About the third hour he went out and saw others standing in the marketplace doing nothing. He told them, 'You also go and work in my vineyard, and I will pay you whatever is right.' So they went.

"He went out again about the sixth hour and the ninth hour and did the same thing. About the eleventh hour he went out and found still others standing around. He asked them, 'Why have you been standing here all day long doing nothing?'

" 'Because no one has hired us,' they answered.

"He said to them, 'You also go and work in my vineyard.'

"When evening came, the owner of the vineyard said to his foreman, 'Call the workers and pay them their wages, beginning with the last ones hired and going on to the first.'

"The workers who were hired about the eleventh hour came and each received a denarius. So when those came who were hired first, they expected to receive more. But each one of them also received a denarius. When they received it, they began to grumble against the landowner. 'These men who were hired last worked only one hour,' they said, 'and you have made them equal to us who have borne the burden of the work and the heat of the day.'

"But he answered one of them, 'Friend, I am not being unfair to you. Didn't you agree to work for a denarius? Take your pay and go. I want to give the man who was hired last the same as I gave you. Don't I have the right to do what I want with my own money? Or are you envious because I am generous?'

"So the last will be first, and the first will be last."

Matthew 20:1-16

Chapter 3

The Difficulty
of Accepting
God's Grace

At an African mission school, many of the boys came from extremely poor homes, which was shown in the rags they had to wear. They were humiliated by the difference between their rags and the clothing worn by

Discovery Point:

Grace defies logic.

students from more wealthy families. To ease their lot, the missionaries decided to provide each boy with a khaki shirt and a pair of khaki shorts, and the local Indian tailor was given an order to make them.

For whatever reason, the tailor made about two-thirds of the shorts with pockets and the remaining shorts without them—all completely free of charge. The boys took the clothing with broad smiles and returned to their dormitories to try them on. A half hour later one-third of the students were lined up in front of the home of the missionary who had issued the clothing. They were no longer smiling.

The missionary came out and asked, "Is something wrong? Can I help you?"

"We have been cheated!" they accused.

"In what way?" he asked.

"Because the other boys got pockets in their shorts and we didn't."

The missionary asked "How much did you pay for your shorts?"

"Why nothing," they replied.

"Then how can you possibly have been cheated?" he wanted to know. "You received a free gift. Why be upset because someone else got more than you did?"

Parable of the Workers in the Vineyard Matthew 20:1-16

Jesus, too, tells of a group of workers who felt cheated. A landowner was seeking people to work in his vineyard. During the course of the day, he went out five different times and hired groups of men to work for him. The place where he looked for employees was the marketplace—that area in a village or town where people met to buy, sell, and trade news of the day. Here the marketplace symbolizes where people are in the ordinary course of their lives.

It is important to note that the prospective workers did not go out looking for the landowner; he went out looking for them. Since the landowner undoubtedly represents Christ, the situation is in keeping with Jesus' statement in Luke 19:10 that "the Son of Man came to seek and to save what was lost."

The Gospel Is for All

In a marketplace was a mixed crowd of people— different races, ages, and places of life. We might conclude from this setting that the gospel was ultimately meant for everyone, everywhere, in every age. However, the marketplace was not identified as the place where the landowner found the earliest groups of workmen. A possible significance in that fact is this: If it were the place where he found all the workers, he would have likely said so at the beginning of the story.

Although Jesus' invitation to "take my yoke upon you" in Matthew 11:29 is a universal call, it was not issued to all men at the same time. He told his disciples to "be my witnesses in Jerusalem, and in all Judea and Samaria, and to the ends of the earth" (Acts 1:8). God's order of priority in preaching the gospel was "first for the Jew, then for the Gentile" (Romans 1:16). When Jesus sent out the twelve apostles for the first time, he said, "Do not go among the Gentiles or enter any town of the Samaritans. Go rather to the lost sheep of Israel" (Matthew 10:5, 6).

Earned Reward?

Therefore, it is suggested that the first group of workmen the Lord sent into his vineyard were Jews who had accepted him as the Messiah, and he was emphasizing a problem not peculiar to, but characteristic of, his Jewish followers. They had been brought up under a strict schoolmaster—the Law of Moses, which said that "the man who does these things will live by them" (Galatians 3:12; Leviticus 18:5). Jesus had met this attitude of meritorious reward twice just before he told this parable. First, the wealthy young man had asked him, "Teacher, what good thing must I do to get eternal life?" (Matthew 19:16). That statement and question had provoked Peter to say, "We have left everything to follow you! What then will there be for us?" (Matthew 19:27).

The application of the Law, which was basically

spiritual and good (Romans 7:12-14), had become increasingly strict and meticulous. This was especially true under the traditional view of the Pharisees during the time just before the ministry of Jesus. In practice, the Law had become a set of tedious rules that made life hard for the conscientious Jew. It emphasized the form of the rule rather than its intent. It required Jewish obedience to the Law code, often including additional rules that went far beyond the intent of the Law itself. But these extended rules usually ignored the Law's real principle and human interests. This gave a careful law keeper a feeling of self-worth based upon his meritorious works. The biggest obstacle that a Jewish follower of Christ had to overcome was accepting the grace of God, instead of claiming what he thought was his earned right to the kingdom. In the words of Paul, "They did not know the righteousness that comes from God and sought to establish their own" (Romans 10:3).

The gospel was ultimately meant for everyone, everywhere, in every age.

Later this caused a problem in the church. The Jews believed that they had "borne the burden of the work and the heat of the day" (Matthew 20:12). Therefore they thought the Samaritans and Gentiles should not be offered salvation without first meeting the requirements of the Law, especially circumcision, as the Jews had been required to do. Many Jewish Christians didn't understand the Gentiles getting "so much for so little," which led to the Jerusalem conference of Acts 15:1-29.

Tax collectors and harlots found it easier to accept
the gospel than the strict Pharisees did (Matthew
21:31, 32). A Samaritan, who felt he had no claim
upon God, was humbly grateful for his money. Jews
accepted blessings as their right and didn't bother to
say thank you (Luke 17:11-18). A Greek woman,
knowing that she was unworthy of the gospel,
begged only for the "crumbs that fell from the table"
(Mark 7:25-30). When the disciples later preached
the gospel to the Mediterranean world, the Gentiles
received it gladly, which angered the Jews and filled
them with jealousy (Acts 13:44-52).

A Salaried Position

Matthew 20:2 shows clearly that the first workmen called would not agree to work until they knew
how much they were going to be paid. The use of the
Greek work *sumphoneo* for "agreed" implies a negotiated contract. There is no mention that the master
was reluctant to meet their demands, or that they
were in any way dissatisfied with the salary he
offered. Nor is it anywhere implied that they failed
to give an honest day's labor as they had undertaken
to do. On the other hand, the contractual agreement
was hardly one of trust.

The other four groups of workmen obviously made
no demands for a set wage. The landowner had
reserved the right to pay them "whatever is fair" and
they had trusted in his honor and truthfulness to
take good care of them. Submitting to the grace of
their master, they were not disappointed, receiving
more than they deserved because the master had
chosen to be generous with his blessings. Faith in
his goodness was more than justified. They knew
well that they had not really earned what they were
given.

It was quite the reverse with the first group. They

had agreed to and received a reasonable wage for
their day's work. But when they saw other workers,
who had not worked the full day, were also paid for
the entire day, they became angry at the grave
injustice. It galled them that the last-hired workmen
had not even had to endure the heat of the midday
sun. They began to complain that they had been
treated unfairly. Not so, replied the landowner. They
had received exactly what they had agreed to and
had worked for. The fact that other workmen had
been paid more than they had worked for was no
concern of theirs. The gracious reward the master
had given the other workmen who had trusted his
goodness was his own money given entirely as he
wanted.

The situation might, in a limited way, be compared to hiring salaried employees today. A salary is
a set amount of money for a defined job, regardless
of the hours required to do the job. No extra money
is earned for overtime work, and no deduction of
money is required if the job is done in fewer than
normal hours. The salary contract is negotiated
between the employer and the employee alone and is
not based on the salaries other employees have
negotiated. Even in today's business world, two
employees comparing salaries for work required can
often cause grumbling and unrest. Some things
never change.

Sharing the Grace

The first-century Jews were eagerly expecting the
kingdom of the Messiah. Since they had maintained
a covenant relationship with God for fifteen centuries, had tithed their possessions, and had observed
the fasts and holy days, they felt that they had
earned a place in the kingdom. Their satisfaction

quickly turned to outrage when they learned that Samaritans and Gentiles were going to share blessings to which they were in no way entitled. Because God in his boundless mercy chose to extend his grace to men who were not descendants of Abraham, many Jews were offended and refused to enter the kingdom. Many who did accept the gospel still harbored injured feelings and only grudgingly agreed that "God has granted even the Gentiles repentance unto life" (Acts 11:18). Some of them, with a deeper understanding of grace, praised God for his mercy to all nations and accepted their Gentile brethren. Most, however, rejected altogether a salvation that had to be shared with others.

Grumblers Get Grace Too

A remarkable point made in the parable is that the grumblers were paid what they believed they had earned. The implication is this: In spite of the imperfect and judgmental view many Jewish Christians had of God's grace, that grace still covered them if they submitted to God's will on the basis of Christ's blood. They hadn't really earned anything, of course. Their salvation, just like the salvation of Samaritans and Gentiles, was entirely an unearned gift of God's grace. Man's work is a *response* to God's grace and not the *basis* of it. Paul sets the relationship between God's grace and man's works in proper focus in Ephesians 2:8-10: "For it is by grace you have been saved, through faith—and this not from yourselves, it is the gift of God—not by works, so that no one can boast. For we are God's workmanship, created in Christ Jesus to do good works, which God prepared in advance for us to do."

The challenge for you, as a Christian, is to search your own soul for the answer to the question of grace versus works salvation: Why do you really do what you do for the church? Do you serve God out of a heart so full of gratitude for his grace that has saved you already? Or do you work for God in order to stay on his good side in hopes that he will weigh your good works and find you deserving of salvation when you die? The first response yields a life of joy and peace; the second response yields a life of fear and weariness. The choice is yours.

Works of service to God are responsive and not meritorious. As James points out in James 2:26, saving faith cannot exist without works. It is like a burning lamp that cannot exist without giving off light. If there is no light, you know the lamp is empty. True faith can no more survive without expressing itself in serving God than the human body can sustain life without breathing.

Are we more like the hypocritical Pharisees of the New Testament than we want to admit? The irony is that God knows our hearts, and he offers us salvation by his glorious grace, free of charge, even if we think we are "first" in his sight. The fact is, we will be last (which equals lost) if we continue placing our hope in what we do rather than who he is. Salvation cannot be earned; it is the gracious gift of our loving Father. It defies logic.

Pharisees—above Repentance?

Jesus, like John the Baptizer, preached in a religious climate poisoned with meticulous but shallow pretense to piety. The dominant moral and philosophical influence in the spiritual life of first-century Jews was pharisaism. It was characterized by rigid adherence to an elaborate expansion of the original Law but did nothing to ennoble the heart and mind or increase concern for others. The term *Pharisee* was really used in two widely differing senses. In a general sense the vast majority of the Jewish population of Palestine were Pharisees. That is, they did not agree with the Sadducees that angels and spirits do not exist, and they believed in a resurrection. They also accepted as authoritative the entire canon of the Hebrew scripture, whereas the Sadducees accepted only the Torah, the five books of Moses. However, the term *Pharisee* as used in the gospels refers to an elite inner circle of very strict and self-righteous religious leaders. These were the Pharisees of the Pharisees, an exclusive sect who not only despised Gentiles as "dogs in the marketplace" but even ordinary, illiterate fellow Jews whom they dismissed as ignorant of the law and incapable of repentance. Their devotion to God was an outward facade of fasting and ritual prayers that masked, unrepentant hearts. Jesus said to them, "You hypocrites! You are like whitewashed tombs, which look beautiful on the outside but on the inside are full of dead men's bones and everything unclean" (Matthew 23:27).

Pearl of Wisdom:

The grace of God defies human logic. It was not logical to the Law-bound Pharisees of Jesus' day, nor is it logical today to those of us who work in order to be saved, rather than work out of gratitude to God because we are saved by his grace.

Focusing Your Faith

1. What is the most valuable lesson you learned from this chapter for your own life?

2. This statement was made in the chapter: "The biggest obstacle that a Jewish follower of Christ had to overcome was accepting the grace of God." Why is this statement still so relevant to followers of Christ today?

3. How do you bring the truth of this statement into your own life: "Man's work is a *response* to God's grace and not the *basis* of it"?

4. Why do people who fully accept the grace of God seem so much more relaxed and happy than those who struggle with this biblical concept?

5. What could your life become if you fully accepted the fact that, because of your obedient faith, God's grace has already saved you? What would change in your life?

6. If you were having a one-on-one conversation with the apostle Paul about God's grace, what do you think you would hear him say to you?

7. You are a student in an art class, and the teacher has asked you to paint a picture of the grace of God. What would it look like? What colors would you use?

Parable of the Unmerciful Servant

Then Peter came to Jesus and asked, "Lord, how many times shall I forgive my brother when he sins against me? Up to seven times?"

Jesus answered, "I tell you, not seven times, but seventy-seven times.

"Therefore, the kingdom of heaven is like a king who wanted to settle accounts with his servants. As he began the settlement, a man who owed him ten thousand talents was brought to him. Since he was not able to pay, the master ordered that he and his wife and his children and all that he had be sold to repay the debt.

"The servant fell on his knees before him. 'Be patient with me,' he begged, 'and I will pay back everything.' The servant's master took pity on him, canceled the debt and let him go.

"But when that servant went out, he found one of his fellow servants who owed him a hundred denarii. He grabbed him and began to choke him. 'Pay back what you owe me!' he demanded.

"His fellow servant fell to his knees and begged him, 'Be patient with me, and I will pay you back.'

"But he refused. Instead, he went off and had the man thrown into prison until he could pay the debt. When the other servants saw what had happened, they were greatly distressed and went and told their master everything that had happened.

"Then the master called the servant in. 'You wicked servant,' he said, 'I canceled all that debt of yours because you begged me to. Shouldn't you have had mercy on your fellow servant just as I had on you?' In anger his master turned him over to the jailers to be tortured, until he should pay back all he owed.

"This is how my heavenly Father will treat each of you unless you forgive your brother from your heart."

Matthew 18:21-35

Chapter 4

Forgiving
from the
Heart

In the year 1818, Tamatoe, king of Huahine, one of the South Sea Islands, became a Christian. Soon afterward, he discovered a vicious plot among his fellow natives to seize him and other converts to Christianity and burn them to death.

Discovery Point:

Forgiving others is essential to my forgiveness.

Tamatoe organized a band of soldiers and ambushed the plotters, capturing them unawares and without violence. He then set a huge feast before them at his banquet tables. It was a gesture of forgiveness and a demonstration of the forgiveness of Christ.

This unexpected kindness by Tamatoe surprised the native savages, who burned their idols and became Christians, too. The power of forgiveness is awesome.

Parable of the Unmerciful Servant Matthew 18:21-35

Jesus points out the powerful effects of forgiveness in his story about a king and his servant. The immeasurable depths of God's mercy and love are contrasted with the meanness of man in this parable. In the story, a king was ready to settle accounts with his servants. A man was brought before him who owed him a huge debt. The amount was stated as 10,000 talents, a sum so overwhelming that it would have been impossible to repay it. The expected response from the debtor is that he could not pay. The king ordered that not only the man's property but even his wife and children had to be sold to repay the debt. The poor wretch fell to his knees and begged for mercy, promising that in time he would repay the debt completely. Perhaps he was just stalling for time; perhaps he really thought he would eventually be able to repay the staggering sum. The king, of course, knew that it was completely unrealistic to expect that the debtor could ever repay what was owed. Nevertheless, in an act of mercy he paid the debt himself by cancelling it altogether.

Up to that point, the parable was a beautiful story of God's boundless forgiveness, but then the tale took a sorry turn. The forgiven servant had scarcely left his master's presence before he saw a fellow servant who owed him a sum that was tiny next to the huge debt which had just been settled for him. His reaction was immediate and angry. He grabbed the poor man by the throat and began choking him while he demanded that the servant pay him in full what he was owed. Like he himself had done shortly before, the man fell to his knees and begged for a little more time. His pleading was to no avail. The creditor charged the man with debt default and had him imprisoned.

Their fellow servants were indignant over the callousness of the first servant and reported his cruelty to their master, the king. The kindly king, who had dealt so leniently with the first man, was incensed at his cruel behavior and had him jailed until the huge debt he had originally owed (and now owed again) was paid.

How Many Times?

This wonderful parable was told due to a question Peter had asked Jesus: "Lord, how many times shall I forgive my brother when he sins against me? Up to seven times?"

Jesus replied, "Not seven times, but seventy-seven times" (Matthew 18:21, 22).

The context of Peter's question suggests that there was no question that he would be sinned against: "*When* he sins against me." But it is not clear why Peter thought that seven times would be enough. Perhaps he based it upon Jesus' statement recorded in Luke 17:3, 4 that one should forgive his brother seven times a day if he repented.

Perhaps he was thinking of the rabbi's teaching on forgiveness based upon Amos chapters 1 and 2. God did not act against the kingdoms listed there until they had committed the fourth transgression. Whatever the background of Peter's question, he clearly thought he was being very generous in suggesting that he would be willing to forgive injury seven times. He must have been startled and embarrassed when Jesus raised the total so high.

It must have been obvious to all the disciples that Jesus did not mean a specific number but was simply saying, "You forgive your brother as often as he sincerely asks you." Peter's question implied a reasonable limit to forgiveness. Jesus' answer removed all limits. How fortunate for us that the limit of forgiveness is not seven or any multiple of it! Otherwise, the remission of our sins would be only a very temporary fix.

Forgiveness Is Conditional

The parable that follows Peter's questions reinforced the principle Jesus had already stated in the prayer he had taught his disciples in Matthew 6:9-13 and his following comment in verses 14, 15. God's forgiveness of us is conditional upon our own forgiveness of others. Only impenitent, unreformed people nurse grudges and seek vengeance.

A deeper dimension is added to this parable when we see forgiveness as one of the ways God communicates his nature to us. He is unwilling for unforgiven sins to create and maintain a gap between him and man. He does not "want anyone to perish" (2 Peter 3:9), so he paid the enormous price of the cross to bring forgiveness to all who would accept it. This is accepted, if not fully understood, by virtually all Christians. But what we sometimes fail to appreciate is that Jesus did not die upon the cross just to remove a barrier between people and God but also to remove the barrier between people. He died to make peace (Ephesians 2:14-16). When we do not forgive each other, we completely devalue the Crucifixion.

We tend to think of kindness and generosity in terms of physical needs: feeding the hungry, clothing the naked, and tending the sick (Matthew 25:35-46). But often greater needs exist in emotional and social areas. We all accept that failing to feed the hungry when we are able to help, robs a fellow human being of something God requires us to give. But one of the greatest needs a person ever has is the blessing of forgiveness. Jesus' principle of judgment especially applies to our merciful treatment of one another: "Whatever you did not do for one of the least of these, you did not do for me." When we do not forgive someone else, we are looking with defiance into the suffering eyes of Christ upon the cross who died to break down such barriers between people. Our sinful selfishness, in fact, drives the nails through his bleeding hands all over again. After all, the world's need for forgiveness is what hung him there in the first place.

A small "bitter root" (Hebrews 12:15) can spread and cause eternal damage. Hostility between Sarah and Hagar over a fight between their sons (Genesis 21:9, 10) has echoed down through history and is still a source of hostility in the Middle East today. How many lives could have been saved and how much misery averted had those two women and boys simply forgiven each other? Each of us has an outstanding debt to forgive every grievance, real or fancied, that we have ever experienced at the hands of another. For "if you do not forgive men their sins, your Father will not forgive your sins" (Matthew 6:15).

> ### *One of the greatest needs a person ever has is the blessing of forgiveness.*

Corinthian Christians were considered spiritually immature because they could not forgive an injury done to them but would prosecute the offending brother in a Roman court of law. Paul asked them, "Why not rather be wronged? Why not rather be cheated?" (1 Corinthians 6:7).

Fortunately, the fate of the city of Nineveh did not rest upon Jonah's personal forgiveness. Israel, God's people had suffered so many indignities at the hands of the Assyrians that the prophet would likely have

destroyed Nineveh down to the smallest infant.
When the Assyrians repented, their old ledger of
wrongs was burned and a new ledger opened in the
tribunal of God. Jonah was outraged at their being
so easily forgiven by God. And yet, forgiven they
were. God is not concerned with what men have
been, but with what they are and want to be.

The Lesson

There are two principal points to this parable. The
first is the enormity of God's grace in forgiving our
sins. Sin is absolutely opposite to the nature and
holiness of God. So, it creates a gulf between the
sinner and the Creator so wide that only love and
patience beyond human understanding can span it.
God and sin are like giant magnets that repel each
other and cannot come together. Only a divine plan
conceived and executed by God himself could make
reconciliation with lost humanity possible. Unless
we can even dimly understand God's utter hatred for
and complete incompatibility with sin, we cannot
begin to understand why his Son had to come to
earth and die on our behalf.

The second point is that although people were
created in the image of God, we have defaced that
image to the point where our inhumanity toward
other human beings has become the expected norm.
We plead for mercy for ourselves but often refuse to
freely extend it to our neighbors. When faced with
the choice of being punished by men or by God, King
David wisely exclaimed, "Let us fall into the hands
of the Lord, for his mercy is great; but do not let me
fall into the hands of men" (2 Samuel 24:14). Jesus
made it clear that a much higher level of godliness is
expected and required of his disciples than prevails
in the world around us: "From everyone who has
been given much, much will be demanded; and from

the one who has been entrusted with much, much more will be asked" (Luke 12:48). Resentment and real or imagined grievances are often the source of disunity and strife in the body of Christ. But when we allow the Spirit of God and the love of Christ to reign in our hearts, these roots of bitterness are removed forever. Paul urged the Ephesian Christians to "get rid of all bitterness, rage and anger, brawling and slander, along with every form of malice. Be kind and compassionate to one another, forgiving each other, just as in Christ God forgave you" (Ephesians 4:31, 32).

The Pattern

Christ set a pattern for our forgiving others when he gave up his very life in order to forgive us. (See Colossians 3:13 and Ephesians 4:32.) We, too, must give up parts of our lives in order to forgive others. We have to give up anger, resentment, hurt feelings, righteous indignation, and hate. We have to give up retaliations, such as not speaking to someone, innu-endos, and saying, "I've forgiven her, but I won't forget it." These actions and feelings are telltale signs that forgiveness has not reached the heart.

God commanded us to forgive one another, not just as a legal statute or peace-keeping rule, but for our own benefit. Harboring resentment and hatred have proven damaging to physical and emotional health. It handicaps your ability to have and hold important relationships, to properly raise children, or to keep a job.It destroys both health and happiness, for happi-ness and health cannot coexist with unhealthy hatred and resentment. True forgiveness, on the other hand, is accompanied by God's eternal promise of great joy and contentment. It is a free-flowing fountain of peace and joy and unity.

The Awesome Application

The unforgiving servant suffered the loss of the forgiveness his gracious lord had already extended to him when he dealt harshly with his fellow servant. The application of that is awesome in our lives. Although God's forgiveness is absolute and total in its scope, erasing every sin entirely, his forgiveness is conditional. Unless we extend the genuine love to each other that "keeps no record of wrongs" (1 Corinthians 13:5), unless we "bear with each other and forgive whatever grievances [we] may have against one another," then we do not "forgive as the Lord forgave [us]" (Colossians 3:13). And the stern warning Jesus gave in Matthew 6:15 becomes effective: "If you do not forgive men their sins, your Father will not forgive your sins."

Pearl of Wisdom:

*Truly and freely forgiving
others is absolutely essential for
us in order for God to forgive us.
Why? God wants us to realize
the magnitude of the gift of his
Son—the price he paid for our
forgiveness. "He who has been
forgiven little loves little;" he
who is forgiven much, loves
much (Luke 7:47).*

Focusing Your Faith

1. How does it make you feel to know that God's forgiveness of you is affected by your own forgiveness of others?

2. How would you solve the problem of forgiving someone who didn't even know or care that they had hurt you and, so, did not ask for forgiveness?

3. Think of someone you know who needs to be encouraged to forgive another person. Decide how you can encourage them. Then do it.

4. Why is this statement true: "When we do not forgive each other, we completely devalue the Crucifixion"?

5. If you heard an admitted alcoholic tearfully ask for forgiveness over and over again, how would you react after the eighth or ninth time?

6. Visualize yourself at the foot of the cross looking into the suffering eyes of Jesus. Next to you is someone who needs your forgiveness. What do you see happening as the scene unfolds?

7. Make a list of people that you need to forgive, in any measure whatsoever, and for what.

Parable of the Friend at Midnight

Then he said to them, "Suppose one of you has a friend, and he goes to him at midnight and says, 'Friend, lend me three loaves of bread, because a friend of mine on a journey has come to me, and I have nothing to set before him.'

"Then the one inside answers, 'Don't bother me. The door is already locked, and my children are with me in bed. I can't get up and give you anything.' I tell you, though he will not get up and give him the bread because he is his friend, yet because of the man's boldness he will get up and give him as much as he needs.

"So I say to you: Ask and it will be given to you; seek and you will find; knock and the door will be opened to you. For everyone who asks receives; he who seeks finds; and to him who knocks, the door will be opened.

"Which of you fathers, if your son asks for a fish, will give him a snake instead? Or if he asks for an egg, will give him a scorpion? If you then, though you are evil, know how to give good gifts to your children, how much more will your Father in heaven give the Holy Spirit to those who ask him!"

Luke 11:5-13

Chapter 5

What Do You Expect

from Prayer?

A Christian missionary was discussing religion with a Hindu friend. In the course of their conversation the missionary asked, "Why do you always beat a gong when you enter your temple?" The Hindu

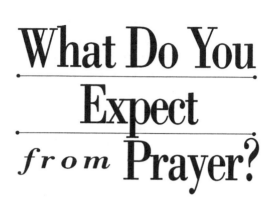

Discovery Point:

God always answers me quickly.

was embarrassed. "You're not going to believe this, but we do it to get our god's attention." Christians are blessed in having a heavenly Father who is always listening for our requests (Psalm 33:18).

George M. Scott, pioneer missionary to Northern Rhodesia (now called Zambia) used to delight in telling this story:

Scott and his wife had made their home into an orphanage for children of all colors. They operated on very little money, as was usually the case with missionaries in the 1920s. They found themselves

$500 in debt—a huge sum in those days. Being a
man of great faith who truly believed that God
always answers the prayers of his children, George
Scott prayed to God for $500. On his next trip to the
trading post, he found an envelope from America in
his mailbox. Upon opening it, he found that it contained a check for $500 and nothing more—no
explanation, no return address, just the check. Scott
was not surprised at this answer to his prayer,
although mildly taken aback at the check being for
the exact amount. Earnestly thanking God for
answering his prayers, he took the money and paid
off his creditors. Since a letter took several months
to travel between America and Africa, Scott realized
the Lord had granted his request a long time before
he made it!

God is always on top of things and has a perfect timetable.

A few days later a second letter came. It was from
the person who had sent the check. It explained that
he had failed to enclose the letter telling George
Scott to divide the money with all his fellow missionaries. By that time, Scott had managed to trade
some cattle and so was able to grant the donor's
request to distribute the money. His interpretation
of the sequence of events was this: God is always on
top of things and has a perfect timetable. He always
hears our prayers and answers them in the way best
for us.

God's covenant people have always made prayer a
central part of their lives. Even before the Egyptian
bondage, the Hebrews were a praying people.
Abraham and his servants were accustomed to

asking God's blessings and guidance (Genesis 20:17, 24:12-14). Moses, David, Job, and Ezra are especially mentioned in connection with their prayers to God. The beautiful prayers of Hannah, Solomon, and David (many Psalms are prayers) are recorded.

So prayer is also treated in a significant way in the teachings of Jesus. Prayer was an important part of Jesus' own life. He taught and encouraged his disciples to pray and inspired them by his own example. He sometimes spent the whole night in prayer (Luke 6:12). His last hours of freedom on earth were spent in prayer (John 17).

Parable of the Friend at Midnight Luke 11:5-13

One of Jesus' parables which makes up part of his teaching on prayer is found in Luke and is commonly known as the parable of the friend at midnight. It has most often been thought to mean we should persist in prayer, since the man asking for bread did not have his request granted until he had insisted at some length that his friend give him what he asked.

This parable was told by Jesus when his disciples asked that he teach them how to pray. First he gives them an example of prayer—a brief prayer of praise, request, and intercession. His brief prayer sharply contrasted the long prayers the disciples usually heard from the Pharisees (Mark 12:40).

Jesus then tells a story about making a request. A man has an unexpected guest arrive late in the evening to spend the night. The visitor has not had supper, but the host has no bread in the house. Rules of hospitality demand that he make some effort to get some. Although it is midnight, he goes to a friend's house and requests that his friend get up and share his bread with him. The friend is annoyed and protests that he is already tucked in his blankets

with his children. He refuses to get up and get the
bread. The friend is, however, not put off and continues making his demands. The man sees that he is
not going to get any sleep until he answers. So he
gets up and gets the bread for his tormentor in order
to get rid of him. What friendship alone could not do,
dogged persistence did.

This parable is usually said to mean that if you
keep praying long enough, although God at first
refused to grant your request, he will certainly give

He is ready (even eager) to do what his children ask.

---

in eventually. There is another view which more
nearly fits the description in the Scriptures of God:
He is ready (even eager) to do what his children ask.
God says this of himself in Isaiah 65:24: "Before they
call I will answer; while they are still speaking I will
hear." And John assures us this: "if we ask anything
according to his will, he hears us. And if we know
that he hears us—whatever we ask—we know that
we have what we asked of him" (1 John 5:14, 15).

Saying Luke 11:5-13 teaches that God must be
worn down by persistent prayer before he will answer lessens the majestic kindness of our loving
Creator. That is not to say that God will not delay
granting a request for his own reasons. It is not to
say that he does not welcome our continuing
prayers, as long as our repetition does not come from
our lack of faith that he heard us the first time.
Jesus points out in Matthew 6:7, 8 that repetitive
prayers nagging God are quite unnecessary, since
"your Father knows what you need before you ask
him."

The usual interpretation says that the parable of the friend at midnight is a lesson on persistence. That's based upon a historical mistranslation of the word found in 11:8. The Greek word *anaideia* was translated "importunity" in the King James Version of 1611. Later translations have been influenced by this usage in the King James Version. The word anaideia does not occur elsewhere in the Scriptures. Since there was no passage to compare it to, it was translated by presuming its contextual meaning. Later research has shown that it comes from a root word which means a sense of honor or self-respect. In other words, the person would feel a sense of shame or loss of self-respect by not taking the most honorable course of behavior.[1] Supporting this view is the manner in which Jesus begins the parable (verse 11). He asks, "Which of you . . .?"[2]

Jesus is saying, "Can you imagine the ridiculous situation in which your friend, even in the middle of the night, would offer excuses to keep from giving you bread if you needed it? Why, he could certainly not do it. Even if the bonds of friendship would not compel

•————————————————————————•

[1]*We are indebted to some German scholars for this linguistic research. Joachim Jeremias points out this meaning of* anaideia *in his book* The Parables of Jesus. *Howard Marshall (in* Eerdman's New International Greek Testament Commentary*), says that he is inclined to prefer Jeremias's conclusions on the grounds that the parable is centered on the attitude of the man in bed, and that verse 8 is offering a contrast to the attitude expressed in verse 7.*

[2]*This question demands the answer "not one." He uses the same device in Luke 14:5: "which of you, having a son or an ox that falls into a well on the Sabbath day, will not immediately put him out?" (RSV). The answer has to be, of course, "Not one of us."*

him to grant your request, his own self-respect certainly would." The unspoken indictment is this: "If a
mere human friend would meet your needs, why
would any believer assume that God would not? Is
he less kind or willing to help his children than the
average human being?"

A missionary in Nazareth was teaching this
parable to a class of Arab Christians. He drew the
traditional conclusion that it is teaching persistence
in making our requests. His audience looked startled
and began shaking their heads. The teacher asked
what was wrong. They replied that he had placed an
impossible interpretation on the story. They then
went on to say that their village culture remained
much the same as it had been during the ministry of
Jesus. In a typical village each family takes a turn in
baking loaves of bread for the whole village (often an
extended family). It is normal and expected that a
family needing bread goes to the person who baked
that day to satisfy their needs. The situation is
intensified if one of the families has an unexpected
guest come to his house. In a wider sense he is the
guest of the entire village. If the bread maker of the
day should refuse to provide a loaf for the visitor, not
only he, but the entire village would be disgraced.

Jesus is making the point that God is not reluctant to help but is willing and ready always to bless
his children. So, we should ask in the assurance that
God will honor our requests. We should seek help
knowing that we will find what we need. And we
should knock expecting him to open the door.

Parable of the Unrighteous Judge Luke 18:1-8

The second parable, about the unrighteous judge,
is another of the "contrast" parables. Like the parable of the friend at midnight, it has often been

Parable of the Unrighteous Judge

Then Jesus told his disciples a parable to show them that they should always pray and not give up. He said: "In a certain town there was a judge who neither feared God nor cared about men. And there was a widow in that town who kept coming to him with the plea, 'Grant me justice against my adversary.'

"For some time he refused. But finally he said to himself, 'Even though I don't fear God or care about men, yet because this widow keeps bothering me, I will see that she gets justice, so that she won't eventually wear me out with her coming!' "

And the Lord said, "Listen to what the unjust judge says. And will not God bring about justice for his chosen ones, who cry out to him day and night? Will he keep putting them off? I tell you, he will see that they get justice, and quickly. However, when the Son of Man comes, will he find faith on the earth?"

Luke 18:1-8

Parable of the Pharisee and the Tax Collector

To some who were confident of their own righteousness and looked down on everybody else, Jesus told this parable: "Two men went up to the temple to pray, one a Pharisee and the other a tax collector. The Pharisee stood up and prayed about himself: 'God, I thank you that I am not like other men—robbers, evildoers, adulterers—or even like this tax collector. I fast twice a week and give a tenth of all I get.'

"But the tax collector stood at a distance. He would not even look up to heaven, but beat his breast and said, 'God, have mercy on me, a sinner.'

"I tell you that this man, rather than the other, went home justified before God. For everyone who exalts himself will be humbled, and he who humbles himself will be exalted."

Luke 18:9-14

interpreted to teach persistence. Though you may not receive a response from God upon your initial request, he has his breaking point. If you persist long enough, he will grant what you ask like the judge. This misunderstanding of the point of the parable comes from Jesus' introduction to the parable: "Then Jesus told his disciples a parable to show them that they should always pray and not give up." This point will be addressed later.

In the story, the unrighteous judge is completely self-centered. He does not care about his duty to his Creator nor the welfare of his fellow-human beings. His life denies the two great commandments (Matthew 22:36-40): to love his God and his neighbors.

Don't give up on prayer.

When a widow pleads her case in his court, he simply doesn't want to be bothered with it. Her situation is desperate enough that she cannot afford to drop the case; so, she continues coming to his court and pleading for justice. The judge is finally agitated with her persistence and decides to act on her behalf to get rid of her.

Those who interpret this story to mean persistence is necessary are equating God with the unjust judge. Yet there could be no greater *contrast* than between the self-serving behavior of the judge of the story and the loving care of our heavenly Father. Jesus is certainly not suggesting that the way to get God to act is to wear him down. These questions, following his telling of the parable, establish the vast difference between the unjust judge and the just Judge:

Will not God bring justice for his chosen ones, who cry out to him day and night? The answer to this question is, "He most certainly will." The relative clause "day and night" is not intended to imply that we must pray all day and all night to get justice from God. Rather it assures us that God's court is always open to the requests of his children. This contrasts a human court where a person can only be heard during certain hours. The second question, "Will he keep putting them off?" demands a negative answer: Certainly he will not! Jesus himself answers the question. He says, "I tell you, he will see that they get justice, and quickly."

Any interpretation of these two parables showing God as reluctant to grant our requests is wrong. But that meaning has sometimes been drawn. Why? Because of Luke's statement (18:1) that Jesus told the parable of the unrighteous judge to teach his disciples to always pray and not give up. But Jesus is not teaching persistence of a single request. He is rather encouraging faith in the power of prayer. And he is teaching the importance of an active and ongoing prayer life. He is saying, "Don't give up on prayer. It should be a continuous part of your relationship with God."

Parable of the Pharisee and the Tax Collector Luke 18:9-14

The parable of the Pharisee and the tax collector is also a contrast parable. Unlike the first two parables, however, the contrast is not between a human being and God. It is between two very different men. One is a member of the spiritual elite of Judaism, a Pharisee. The other is a member of that despised profession, tax collector.

By the time of Jesus, one movement had ended in pharisaism. It developed out of the Maccabean resistance to the Greeks who were corrupting the Mosaic religion. Those who gave in to pressure from

their rulers to adopt the Greek language and culture
are called Hellenists. They were labeled by Jews
faithful to the Law as "unbelievers." This division in
Judaism continued in the first century A.D. by the
Pharisees and the Sadducees. The name *Pharisee*
comes from a Hebrew word meaning "clean." They
were, in their own eyes, the "clean" (uncorrupted)
ones.

Like many strict movements, the Pharisees had
become extremely legalistic. They depended upon an
ever-expanding system of detailed rules, which were
supposed to have come from the Law of Moses. In
fact, these rules often violated the very purposes of
the original law. The Pharisees had become highly
self-righteous and critical of all who did not agree
with their harsh, strict system. They considered
themselves as the righteous remnant of the Jewish
people.

The tax collector, on the other hand, was a religious and social outcast. Often in the gospels tax
collectors are lumped together with sinners of harlots as the most ungodly of mankind. There is no
comparison between the tax collector of first century
Palestine and the modern IRS agent. In the first
place, he was an employee of the hated Roman
enemy and, therefore, a traitor to his own people.
But, more importantly, he was not so much a tax
collector as a tax *contractor*. So long as he paid the
Romans the tax due them, he could exact as much
more as he cared from his victims and keep the
difference for himself. They generally grossly abused
their power and were often very rich. They were
bitterly resented and hated by their own people.

So, these two extremes on the scale of piety—a
Pharisee and a tax collector—went up to the temple
to pray. The Pharisee was very comfortable in his
personal righteousness; the tax collector was deeply

convicted of his unworthiness of God's favor.

The Pharisee, Jesus said, prayed about himself. Although he offered thanks to God, it was focused upon his own excellent character. He was so different from the rest of mankind who are robbers, evil doers, adulterers, or tax collectors (like the one standing over there). He cites examples of his godliness: He fasts twice every week and gives a tenth of his income to God.

We may note that in the Pharisee's prayer, he was

- *Egotistical.* He had not come to pray for forgiveness; he felt no need of that.

- *Arrogant.* He had not come to thank God for his gifts of life and health and the necessities of life. He had come to call God's attention to what a righteous person he was.

- *Selfish.* He had not come to ask God's mercy and blessings upon others. He mentions other people only to draw a contrast between them and himself.

- *Ungracious.* He did not suggest that he returned a tenth of the wealth God had given him. He was the giver, not God. He gave God a tithe of what he himself got.

- *Trusting in his own acts of merit.* "I fast twice a week."

Jesus said of him and others like him that they "were confident of their own righteousness and looked down on everybody else." God cannot help a man who cannot see in himself a need for God's mercy and strength.

The tax collector had no illusions about himself. He did not need the Pharisee's help in pointing out that he was a sinner. He made no pretense to any claim upon God's favor. He, unlike the Pharisee, did not call God's attention to any praiseworthy aspects of his character and life style. He had no defense, nothing to offer God except a broken heart. He simply begged for God's mercy.

Jesus ends the story by concluding this: "I tell you that this man [the tax collector], rather than the other [the Pharisee], went home justified before God. For everyone who exalts himself will be humbled, and he who humbles himself will be exalted."

From these three parables on prayer, we learn certain principles about what God expects of us when we come to him with our requests and petitions:

- He expects us to approach him in the full assurance that he is willing and able to answer our prayers.

- He is more concerned with the attitudes of our hearts than he is in the length or number of our prayers.

- He expects us to be humble and honest with him and not use prayer as an opportunity to call his attention to our own good qualities and deeds.

Pearl of Wisdom:

God is a loving Father who listens at a moment's notice and always answers as quickly.

Focusing Your Faith

1. What do you expect from prayer? Make a list of your expectations.

2. When you pray to God, what does he look like to you?

3. Prayer is a life-changing experience. How has it changed your life?

4. How would praying in the same closet with the
    tax collector make you feel? How about standing
    next to the Pharisee?

5. What would your normal response be if you were
    awakened at midnight by a neighbor wanting to
    borrow some bread? Why?

6. What changes do you think would occur if your
    family prayed together for an extended time
    every morning?

7. Sing or write a prayer of praise to God.

Parable of the Shrewd Manager

Jesus told his disciples: "There was a rich man whose manager was accused of wasting his possessions. So he called him in and asked him, 'What is this I hear about you? Give an account of your management, because you cannot be manager any longer.'

"The manager said to himself, 'What shall I do now? My master is taking away my job. I'm not strong enough to dig, and I'm ashamed to beg—I know what I'll do so that, when I lose my job here, people will welcome me into their houses.'

"So he called in each one of his master's debtors. He asked the first, 'How much do you owe my master?'

" 'Eight hundred gallons of olive oil,' he replied.

"The manager told him, 'Take your bill, sit down quickly, and make it four hundred.'

"Then he asked the second, 'And how much do you owe?'

" 'A thousand bushels of wheat,' he replied.

"He told him, 'Take your bill and make it eight hundred.'

"The master commended the dishonest manager because he had acted shrewdly. For the people of this world are more shrewd in dealing with their own kind than are the people of the light. I tell you, use worldly wealth to gain friends for yourselves, so that when it is gone, you will be welcomed into eternal dwellings.

"Whoever can be trusted with very little can also be trusted with much, and whoever is dishonest with very little will also be dishonest with much. So if you have not been trustworthy in handling worldly wealth, who will trust you with true riches? And if you have not been trustworthy with someone else's property, who will give you property of your own?

"No servant can serve two masters. Either he will hate the one and love the other, or he will be devoted to the one and despise the other. You cannot serve both God and Money."

Luke 16:1-13

Chapter 6

Is Money Your God?

O scar Wilde once said, "People do not value sunsets because they cannot pay for them." He may have been all too accurate. Money so distorts our sense of values that in trying

> **Discovery Point:**
>
> *I am called to make the most of what I have.*

to possess it we are transported from the simple beauty of basic truths to the frenzied dance of death.

Parable of the Shrewd Manager Luke 16:1-13

Jesus illustrates the wisdom of well-managed money and assets in his story about a shrewd manager. This parable focuses on far-sighted management. A rich farmer's (or perhaps merchant's) business manager was charged with wasting the owner's assets. He is called to account for mishandling his employer's assets, and, although it is not expressly

stated, the charges were obviously true. He was fired
but given some time to clear up his accounts.

The manager was desperate, as he had no prospect of another good job. He quickly rejected the idea
of hiring out as a manual laborer, knowing that he
would not be physically up to the hard work. His
self-image could not survive the humiliation of
begging. So, he was deeply disturbed about his dire
predicament, until a brilliant idea occurred to him.
Although he would soon be out on the street, he
could still control his future if he acted quickly.
Calling up his employer's debtors, he reduced the
amount they owed his employer by as much as fifty
percent. His motive was to obligate them to himself
by his generosity. Then their honor would oblige
them to help him when he was broke and unem-
ployed. His employer was very impressed by the
manager's wisdom and congratulated him.

Jesus observed that people of the commercial
world show much more common sense in dealing
with each other (that is, in their handling of assets)
than do his own followers (the people of light). He
then advised, "I tell you, use worldly wealth to gain
friends for yourselves, so that when it is gone, you
will be welcomed into eternal dwellings" (Luke 16:9).

Commending the Contemptible?

Many students of the parables have been deeply
troubled by what they think is commendation of an
evil rascal by the manager's master, who they believe represents Jesus himself.

In the first place, the master's commendation is
for the manager's foresight in securing his future,
not necessarily for the means he used to achieve it.
In the second place, the manager's actions may be
misinterpreted if we transfer them out of their
ancient Mideastern context into our twenty-first

century, Western commercial world. Some scholars
of ancient Mideastern culture believe that is just
what has happened.

These scholars say that the person who is called
in Greek the *oikonomos* (manager) was, in fact, a
contractor or business agent who operated on a
flexible commission, much as tax collectors like
Zacchaeus did for the Roman government. In other
words, these agents were bound to collect from
buyers the price their employer required for his
products. But they could charge whatever they
could get above that and keep the difference for
their own commission. Often the profit they made
was enormous.

When we don't share, we are stealing God's possession.

This would explain the unusual favorable reaction from the manager's master. Normally he would
surely have had the manager arrested for fraud.
The owner received what was owed him; the manager simply sacrificed his own short-term profit for
long-term security. This explanation would much
better fit the moral of the parable: Christians
should use their assets in a way that will please
God, so that when they no longer have control of
them, they can look forward to living in the mansion
in heaven that God has prepared for good stewards.
On the other hand, the material things we "own"
don't really belong to us; we just have the use of
them, and any "profit" we make is really his. In
reality we steal from God when we take as our own
what he expects us to use for others. When we don't
share, we are stealing God's possession. The master

here commends the manager for changing his mind
from selfishness to doing something to benefit others. And that's the true attitude change that's required for a godly money manager—from selfishness
to benevolence, from personal gain to helping others.
Jesus continued, "Whoever can be trusted with
very little can also be trusted with much, and whoever is dishonest with very little will also be dishonest with much. So if you have not been trustworthy
in handling worldly wealth, who will trust you with
true riches? And if you have not been trustworthy
with someone else's property, who will give you
property of your own? No servant can serve two
masters. Either he will hate the one and love the
other, or he will be devoted to the one and despise
the other. You cannot serve both God and money"
(verses 10-13).

The "very little" in this verse represents money.
And "true riches" and "much" represent eternal life.

Serving Your God

Jesus uses the Aramaic word *mammon* for money.
The word occurs only in Luke 16:13 and in Matthew
6:24. When Jesus uses the term *mammon* to refer to
wealth, he is giving it a personal and spiritual
character. When he declares, "You cannot serve God
and Money [mammon]" (Matthew 6:24), he is per-
sonifying mammon as a rival god.

In saying this, Jesus is making it unmistakably
clear that money is not just some impersonal me-
dium of exchange. Money is not something that is
simply morally neutral, a source to be used in good
and bad ways depending solely upon our attitude
toward it. Mammon is a power that seeks to domi-
nate. In other words, money has the power to rule
your life if you become its servant.

The rich young ruler asked Jesus how he could

have eternal life. He received the startling reply, "If you want to be perfect, go, sell your possessions and give to the poor, and you will have treasure in heaven. Then come, follow me" (Matthew 19:21). The instruction makes sense only when we see that the rich young ruler's wealth was a rival god seeking his complete devotion. Note that when the young man went away sorrowful, Jesus did not run after him and suggest that he only meant a tenth. No, money had become an all-consuming idol and had to be rejected totally in order for the young man "to have eternal life."

Paul observed, "For the love of money is a root of all kinds of evil" (1 Timothy 6:10). Many have rightly observed that Paul did not say *money* but the *love* of money. Given the almost universal love of money, however, they are often the same in practice. By saying that the love of money is a root of all kinds of evil, he does not mean that money literally produces all evil. He means that there is no kind of evil the person who loves money will not do to get it and hold on to it. All restraint is removed. The lover of money will do anything for it. The person is "hooked" when money is god, like an addict to heroine.

Perhaps we need to stamp everything in our possession with this reminder, "Given by God, owned by God, and to be used for the purposes of God." We need to find ways to remind ourselves over and over again that the earth is the Lord's, not ours.

When we give with glad and generous hearts, we evict the tough old miser that lives within us. Even the poorest of us needs to know that we can give something. Just the very act of letting go of money or some other treasure does something within us. We cannot consistently give money without giving self, and that's good for us.

Unraveling the Mystery

Now let's reconcile Jesus' statement that we cannot serve both God and mammon (Matthew 6:24) with his concern that we are to make friends by means of "unrighteous mammon" (Luke 16:9, RSV).

Our biggest difficulty is with Jesus' own commandments following the parable. He first says, "For the people of this world are more shrewd in dealing with their own kind than are the people of the light" (Luke 16:8). Next Jesus makes a most startling statement, "I tell you, use worldly wealth to gain friends for yourselves, so that when it is gone, you will be welcomed into eternal dwellings." In short, Jesus is telling us to use money in such a way that when it fails—and it will fail—we will still be cared for.

Two things shock us in these words of Jesus. First, money is unrighteous, or worldly. Second, we're to use it to make friends. The two ideas seem so opposed to each other that we find it hard to believe that Jesus could have meant both. The language, however, is clear. He did, indeed, mean exactly what he said.

The potential unrighteousness of money is a hard pill for us to swallow. We so badly want to believe money has no power over us, no authority of its own. But by giving the descriptive adjective "unrighteous" to money, Jesus forbids us from ever taking so naive a view of wealth. He tells us that in money matters the children of this world are wiser than the children of light. They know that money is far from harmless. Money is a subtle poison, and if it is used in the wrong way, it can destroy as few other things can. They also know that once you conquer money and learn how to use it, its power is virtually unlimited.

Money's power is completely out of proportion to

its purchasing power. Because the children of this world understand this, they can use money for non-economic purposes, and use it they do. Money is used as a weapon to bully people to keep them in line. It is used to buy prestige and honor, to enlist the allegiance of others, or to corrupt people. And this is precisely why Jesus tells us to make friends by means of this unrighteous money. Rather than run from money, we are to take it, and use it for God's purposes. Rather than reject it, we are to conquer it, subdue it, and use it for greater goals.

> *Once you conquer money and learn how to use it, its power is virtually unlimited.*

We can now bring into harmony the commandment of Matthew 6 that we are not to serve money, and the counsel of Luke 16 that we are to make friends by means of unrighteous money.

The Christian is given the high calling of *using* money without *serving* money. We are using money when we allow God to determine our economic decisions. We simply must decide who's going to make our decisions—God or money. If money determines what we do and do not do, then money is our master. If God determines what we do or do not do, God is our master.

The conflict we feel between Luke 16:9 and Matthew 6:24 is answered by learning to use money without serving money. But we must not be fooled. In the rough and tumble of life, we find that the conflict is not easily nor quickly resolved. So often those who tried to make friends by using money soon are serving it. We cannot safely use money until we are absolutely clear that we are dealing not just with money, but with potentially *unrighteous* money.

Money Is a Spiritual Issue

It is dishonest not to manage money according to the Master's instructions. He tells us to use it to "buy" friends, doing good for people in his name, since the money we have belongs to him anyway.

Finally, it is important to constantly and fervently pray for guidance in money matters. Money is a spiritual issue, and prayer is our chief weapon in the life of the Spirit. Let us learn to pray for each other for the binding of greed and envy and the releasing of charity and generosity.

It has been well said, "He is no fool who gives what he cannot keep to gain what he cannot lose" (James Elliot).

This study of mammon (possessions) compels us to conclude that Christians are called to view life with a single faith focus: putting the kingdom of God first in our list of priorities. Jesus said, "Seek first his kingdom and his righteousness, and all these things will be given to you" (Matthew 6:33). He was talking about what we eat, what we drive, and what we wear. If we have singleness of purpose (serving God first), then our lives are freed from the complications of trying to reach multiple goals. This singleness of focus enables us to see clearly what is really important in life and to have joy in the simple things God constantly gives us.

"If your eyes are good [lit., If your eye be single, or simple], your whole body will be full of light" (Matthew 6:22). If the eye of the soul has a single focus, it will recognize the things that have real substance and will produce trust in the God who gives them.

The apostle Paul found the key to true happiness.

He told the Philippians (4:11), "I have learned to be content whatever the circumstances." He urged them to "not be anxious about anything" (4:6). Christians are in the happy state of "having nothing and yet possessing everything." And so, Christians do not grasp physical things tightly. They can own possessions without being owned by possessions, because they only hold money in trust until a need for it strips it from their temporary control. The first Christians experienced an exuberant joy with "glad and sincere hearts" (Acts 2:46)—because they were free. They were not just free from condemnation, but they were free from the strangling embrace of the god Mammon. "No one claimed that any of his possessions were his own, but they shared everything they had" (Acts 4:32). Joyful giving is your ultimate weapon in conquering money. If God is truly your God, then you will use his money as he instructed— you will give it away in order that he may multiply it back to you, so you can give it away again doing good in his name.

True Riches

The "true riches" of Jesus' parable obviously represent salvation and eternal life. If these are true riches, then all other riches (money and possessions) must be false riches. They are false because they are temporary.

True riches come to us free of charge through the grace of God when our faith is truly focused on him. "You can't take it with you" is certainly a true statement in regard to the riches of this world—gifts from the god Mammon. True riches, on the other hand, are finally the only real possession we can own.

How we handle or manage the Master's assets while on this earth shows in a powerful way who our God (or god) really is. Money management is a prime indicator of whether you have entrusted your life to God for eternal salvation. Your handling of money shows if you're placing your saving faith in him, or if you have sold your soul to the lessor god Mammon.

The point to remember is that we all *will* serve daily the God or god of our lives by the way we spend our money and time. Our daily decision, then, is whom we will serve.

Pearl of Wisdom:

_How you handle the
money that passes
through your control on
this earth is an accurate
barometer of whether you
are saved or not. Do you
serve the God Almighty
or the "Almighty Dollar"?_

Focusing Your Faith

1. Name at least two new ideas that you gained from this chapter.

2. Why do most people have such a hard time giving liberally to God and others?

3. When you hold a large sum of cash in your hand, what emotions do you feel? Be honest.

4. If your money could talk, what do you think it would say about you?

5. Pretend for a moment that the money you contributed last year became a person. What personality traits did your money-person have?

6. Try an experiment with your giving. Increase your gift to God substantially for a few weeks, making financial cuts in other areas if necessary, and keep track of specific results you see. Be prepared for a surprise.

7. Create a step-by-step, how-to plan for managing your money in a more spiritual way. Share the plan with your family and enlist their support. Pray for God's support too.

Parable of the Good Samaritan

On one occasion an expert in the law stood up to test Jesus. "Teacher," he asked, "what must I do to inherit eternal life?"

"What is written in the Law?" he replied. "How do you read it?"

He answered: " 'Love the Lord your God with all your heart and with all your soul and with all your strength and with all your mind'; and, 'Love your neighbor as yourself.' "

"You have answered correctly," Jesus replied. "Do this and you will live."

But he wanted to justify himself, so he asked Jesus, "And who is my neighbor?"

In reply Jesus said: "A man was going down from Jerusalem to Jericho, when he fell into the hands of robbers. They stripped him of his clothes, beat him and went away, leaving him half dead. A priest happened to be going down the same road, and when he saw the man, he passed by on the other side. So too, a Levite, when he came to the place and saw him, passed by on the other side. But a Samaritan, as he traveled, came where the man was; and when he saw him, he took pity on him. He went to him and bandaged his wounds, pouring on oil and wine. Then he put the man on his own donkey, took him to an inn and took care of him. The next day he took out two silver coins and gave them to the innkeeper. 'Look after him,' he said, 'and when I return, I will reimburse you for any extra expense you may have.'

"Which of these three do you think was a neighbor to the man who fell into the hands of robbers?"

The expert in the law replied, "The one who had mercy on him."

Jesus told him, "Go and do likewise."

Luke 10:25-37

Chapter 7

Loving
t h e
Unloveable

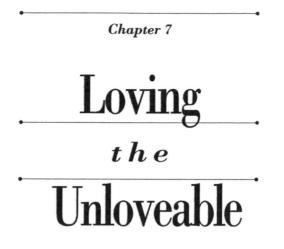

Discovery Point:

Loving others shows my love for God.

A proud Prussian officer of the German Wehrmacht fell into the hands of British troops during World War II. He was badly wounded, so he was taken immediately to a field hospital where it was determined he needed a blood transfusion. As the medical staff set up the transfusion equipment, the wounded Prussian demanded, "Is that British blood?" Upon receiving a yes, he said, "Then I'd rather die!' and he did.

A missionary to India told of seeing a Brahmin (high caste Hindu) who was drowning. He was pulled from the river and saved by an outcast (the lowest class of the caste system). The Brahmin finally recovered enough to speak. Instead of thanking the man who had saved his life, he berated him for his insolence in presuming to touch him.

Anthropologists think that Easter Island was settled by refugees from South America who fled for their lives on balsa rafts. These refugees, known as "the long ears," were escaping from the more dominant people of South America who were short-eared. These long ears were completely unacceptable and were cruelly persecuted in the short-eared society.

These true accounts help us realize that prejudice against people who are different is nothing new. It's as old as life itself.

Parable of the Good Samaritan Luke 10:25-37

Jesus tells a parable of a man who conquers prejudice and does the right thing. Few stories have so moved humanity as the beautiful tale about a Samaritan man who was a good neighbor to a Jew. If the two had met under ordinary circumstances, the Jew would likely have treated him with contempt. So, prejudice was defeated.

The Samaritans had an interesting history. It began with the resettlement of the Northern Kingdom of Israel after the Assyrians had carried off into exile the ten tribes. Immigrants from a number of population centers in Babylonia were settled in Israel by the Assyrian King Sargon. This is referred to in 2 Kings 17:34-40 and confirmed by Sargon's own chronicles.

Ezra 4:2-10 mentions that settlers were also brought in by the Kings Esarhaddon and Ashurbanipal. These Babylonian immigrants had a similar culture to the Israelites, and their language was a northern Semitic language like the Hebrew language of Israel. The great difference between the two peoples was that the Babylonians were idolaters. Sargon sent a Hebrew priest back to Israel to convert them to the religion of Yahweh, God of

Israel, but with limited success. In 2 Kings 17:41 is
the complaint that "even while these people were
worshiping the Lord, they were serving their idols."
The Jews hardly had room for prejudice against the
Samaritans on grounds of idolatry. (See Ezekiel
chapters 8 and 9.) Ironically, the Samaritans kept up
the daily sacrifice to God over 1900 years longer
than the Jews themselves did.

In actual fact, the Assyrians deported only 27,290
Israelites of the northern tribes. A substantial
population of Jacob's children remained behind and
mixed with the Babylonian settlers. The Samaritans
were proud of their descent from Jacob (John 4:12)
and professed to be worshipers of the true God and
so brothers of the Jews themselves (Ezra 4:2). Need-
less to say, the Jewish leaders were not too pleased
at the implied kinship (Ezra 4:3).

Zerubbabel, the Jewish leader of the plan to
rebuild the temple in Jerusalem, curtly refused the
Samaritans' offer of help, although he did not deny
their claim to be worshipers of Yahweh (God). The
Samaritans, thus rejected, built their own temple on
Mt. Gerizim. The resulting hostility still plagued the
relationship between Jews and Samaritans during
the ministry of Jesus.

The occasion for this parable is an ongoing sin of
mankind—prejudice against people who are different from ourselves. We feel threatened by persons
who speak another language, whose skin is a different shade of brown, or whose culture or lifestyle
seems strange to us. Jesus' story of the good Samaritan focuses upon one example of such prejudice in
his time and among his people, but the application
probably fits each of us in one way or another.

Bad Guy/Good Guy

The distaste of the Jewish elite—Pharisees, priests, and scribes—for Samaritans was extreme. Jesus could hardly have picked a character more abrasive and odious to his audience than a Samaritan. And it was particularly offensive that Jesus cast the hated Samaritan in the role of the good guy.

In the wild stretch of broken limestone hills which leads down from Jerusalem to Jericho, violent robbery was not unusual. So, this story began with a well-known happening. Jesus identified the victim of the parable only as "a man," but in this context he could only have been a Jew. Otherwise, Jesus would have named him differently for his Jewish listeners. The point of the parable would have been lost if he were not a Jew. That point is this: any human being who needs our help is our neighbor, however different from ourselves he may be. Such a definition of "neighbor" was necessary because of the implied limitation the lawyer questioning Jesus would naturally attach to the term.

Love of one's neighbor is a genuine heart response to human need. It is not selective on prejudicial basis. Neither is it casual charity motivated by the giver's desire for an enhanced self-image or for someone's approval. When the lawyer asked, "Who is my neighbor?" his silent implication was that we must not make the application too general, or we will find ourselves involved with some very undesirable people. But when we open our hearts to such "aliens," then we display one of God's own attributes, that of impartial love.

Since Jesus' questioner was an expert on the law, he should not have asked such a question, for the law contained abundant teaching on caring for strangers. For example, Deuteronomy 10:16-19

states it powerfully: "Circumcise your hearts, therefore, and do not be stiff-necked any longer. For the
Lord your God is God of gods and Lord of lords, the
great God, mighty and awesome, who shows no
partiality and accepts no bribes. He defends the
cause of the fatherless and the widow, and loves the
alien, giving him food and clothing. And you are to
love those who are aliens, for you yourselves were
aliens in Egypt."

Leviticus 19:33, 34 says it similarly: "When an
alien lives with you in your land, do not mistreat
him. The alien living with you must be treated as
one of your native-born. Love him as yourself, for
you were aliens in Egypt. I am the Lord your God."

Rationalizing Our Actions

But the parable is not concerned just with the
kind Samaritan who went out of his way, at considerable cost in time and money, to help a person who
was an alien to him. It also involves two special
Jews whose calling obligated them to be good examples in obeying the law—a priest and a Levite.
Quite apart from the fact that the victim, lying
naked and wounded by the roadside, was a Jew, they
had a most serious responsibility to minister to him.
At the very least, their own warped sense of duty
should have compelled them to help a fellow Jew.
Instead, they "passed by on the other side." Their
actions suggested that they didn't even want to look
at him closely lest some small spark of human
decency might move them to get involved against
their practical good sense.

What possible motivation could have caused them
to show such callous disregard of human needs?
Some justifying excuses might have been these:

More urgent concerns. Priests and Levites were

important members of the Jewish community. They were responsible for the temple worship and all of its needs. If the Jewish man were dead, and they had touched him, God's own law said they would then have been unclean and could not help with any of the temple services. Surely, people of such public importance should not get involved in what might have turned out to be a time-consuming and unpleasant task. Besides, there would be plenty of other people passing along the road whose priorities were not so urgent as their own.

Personal risk. It was a dangerous stretch of road. The robbers who had attacked the man would certainly not have been far away. And to have remained longer than necessary in the area would have been courting disaster. A party of travelers might have stood a better chance of survival, but a single person would have been at too grave a risk.

Expense and inconvenience. Suppose the man had not recovered sufficiently to walk; how was he to have been carried? It might have involved a long wait until someone else came along to help transport him. One certainly would not have wanted nightfall to overtake him in such a place. Even granting that they could have succeeded in getting him to a hospice in Jericho, who would have paid for his care?

All things considered, it certainly appeared to be the smart course to leave well enough alone. The only problem with remaining uninvolved was that it meant they completely ignored the two great commandments—love God and love your neighbor.

Contemporary Counterparts

A similar situation might arise in America today. A preacher, already late and frustrated, is driving a little above the legal speed limit to get to his pulpit

before the congregation finishes the first hymn. He
sees a stranded woman beside her stalled car on the
roadside frantically waving. His first impulse to stop
is quickly squelched because he doesn't know her.
Surely the spiritual interests of three hundred
people are more important than the personal problem of some nameless woman. The least possible
problem if he stopped would be a flat tire, and that
would involve getting his hands and suit dirty. The
Lord's work must have a greater priority than one
person's need. Besides, there will be plenty of other
cars coming along whose riders are not involved in
church and so have nothing better to do with their
time than to help the woman. He drives on.

The next car to come along, however, is driven by
a Sunday school teacher. He has thirty youngsters
waiting for him to teach them about God's love and
about how he expects his people to love each other.
Faced with the choice, he pushes a little harder on
the accelerator. It is somewhat sobering, however, to
reflect on Jesus' statement: "I tell you the truth,
whatever you did not do for one of the least of these,
you did not do for me" (Matthew 25:45). When we
look into the face of human need, we are looking into
the face of Jesus Christ.

Godliness, Not Duty

Even though the Samaritan of the parable was
obviously going somewhere, he didn't allow anything
to take priority over offering kindness to someone
who desperately needed him. When he saw the
wounded man, he went immediately to him to see
what he could do. He began by dressing the man's
injuries as best he could with oil, wine, and ban-
dages. Then, lifting the man onto his own donkey, he
led him to the nearest inn and arranged for him to
recover there. He paid the innkeeper himself and

assured him that he would pay any more expense when he returned.

No one expected the Samaritan (any Samaritan) to help the Jew (any Jew). In fact, if anyone could have been *expected* to leave the wounded Jew to his fate, it would have been the Samaritan. After all, the Jew would not likely have chosen a Samaritan to help him. In reverse circumstances it is unlikely that the Jew would have helped, or even have spoken to, the Samaritan. The Samaritan showed kindness to the Jew even though . . .

- nobody expected it of him;

- the Jew probably would not have helped him under reversed circumstances;

- he himself had to walk in order for the donkey to carry the Jew;

- he could have just dumped the Jew at the inn and said to the innkeeper, "He's one of yours. What you do with him has nothing to do with me."

Accepting the Challenge

Jesus' parting charge to the lawyer to "go and do likewise" is troubling. It suggests that there are things much more basic to our relationship to God than simply "playing church." Unless a Christian's total lifestyle reflects genuine love for his God and his neighbor, all of his sermons, hymns, and prayers are nothing more than "a resounding gong or a clanging cymbal" (1 Corinthians 13:1).

Agape love is something you do for someone, not something you necessarily feel. This active love can be demonstrated only by loving our neighbors—even the unloveable ones. Loving others is the only avenue God has given us to love him. This, of course, is the reason the second greatest commandment is like the first: "Love your neighbor as yourself" (Matthew 22:39). This is also why 1 John is so emphatic when it says, "If anyone says, 'I love God' yet hates his brother, he is a liar" (1 John 4:20).

> ### Loving others is the only avenue God has given us to love him.

Agape love is doing the unexpected, the unnatural, sometimes the socially unacceptable thing for someone who may even be unloveable. It is doing the loveable thing without necessarily feeling love. That is how you really show your love for God—by allowing his unprejudiced love for all people to demonstrate itself to the world through you, thus drawing men and women to the love of the God who lives in you. If you only show love when you feel love, that's not godliness, that's only humanness. There's nothing unusual or uniquely Christian in that—nothing to help people see God in action.

Agape love is not an emotional feeling. Most Christians recognize that as a fact, but we do not know how to replace our view of love with this true meaning. We must learn that it means being concerned about the well-being of another person, whether we like them or not. When we finally grasp this understanding, the puzzling command for us to "love our enemies" (as the Samaritan did the Jew) becomes doable by us mere humans.

The Real Point

Our assurance of salvation is closely tied to our being a living example of God's agape love—unprejudiced love in action. We are foolish to say we are saved by the grace of God and, yet, rarely demonstrate the loving spirit of that same God by loving our neighbors and, thus, loving him. That only shows we are not yet truly in touch with the magnitude of the love of God in redeeming us through Christ.

The old cartoon character, Hambone, used to sum it up nicely when he quipped, "There ain't no use saying you love God when you ain't speakin' to your neighbor."

Pearl of Wisdom:

Loving others, even the unloveable, is the only way God has provided for us to love him. If we can't or don't love others, we can't love him.

Focusing Your Faith

1. How can love be either an emotional or a non-emotional response?

2. If Jesus taught this parable in your town today, who do you think he would use as the story's characters instead of Jews and Samaritans?

3. What would our country become if everyone "loved his neighbor" as the Samaritan did?

4. Put yourself in the place of the Samaritan in this parable. What feelings do you experience when you realize a person who hates you needs your help?

5. Why do you think God commanded us to love our neighbors or, even more difficult, to love our enemies? What do we learn about God when we do this?

6. Imagine a conversation between the Samaritan and the Jew in this story. What are the first things you hear them say to each other?

7. When you see someone in need of help, how does the person's appearance (race, clothing, cleanliness, status, etc.) affect the way you normally respond? Compare your usual response to God's request that you "love your neighbor."

Parable of the Talents

"Again, it will be like a man going on a journey, who called his servants and entrusted his property to them. To one he gave five talents of money, to another two talents, and to another one talent, each according to his ability. Then he went on his journey. The man who had received the five talents went at once and put his money to work and gained five more. So also, the one with the two talents gained two more. But the man who had received the one talent went off, dug a hole in the ground and hid his master's money.

"After a long time the master of those servants returned and settled accounts with them. The man who had received the five talents brought the other five. 'Master,' he said, 'you entrusted me with five talents. See, I have gained five more.'

"His master replied, 'Well done, good and faithful servant! You have been faithful with a few things; I will put you in charge of many things. Come and share your master's happiness!'

"The man with the two talents also came. 'Master,' he said, 'you entrusted me with two talents; see, I have gained two more.'

"His master replied, 'Well done, good and faithful servant! You have been faithful with a few things; I will put you in charge of many things. Come and share your master's happiness!'

"Then the man who had received the one talent came. 'Master,' he said, 'I knew that you are a hard man, harvesting where you have not sown and gathering where you have not scattered seed. So I was afraid and went out and hid your talent in the ground. See, here is what belongs to you.'

"His master replied, 'You wicked, lazy servant! So you knew that I harvest where I have not sown and gather where I have not scattered seed? Well then, you should have put my money on deposit with the bankers, so that when I returned I would have received it back with interest.

" 'Take the talent from him and give it to the one who has the ten talents. For everyone who has will be given more, and he will have an abundance. Whoever does not have, even what he has will be taken from him. And throw that worthless servant outside, into the darkness, where there will be weeping and gnashing of teeth.' "

Matthew 25:14-30

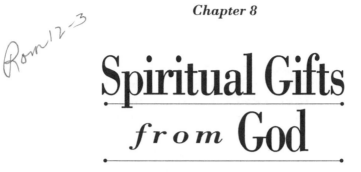

Chapter 8

Spiritual Gifts
from God

Rom 12-3

D uring a church business meeting on a fall Sunday afternoon in Pittsburgh, Pennsylvania, in 1973, church leaders discussed what should be done with the $33,000 savings account the church had in the bank. The treasurer

Discovery Point:

God has a special purpose for me.

said they should just leave it in savings "for a rainy day." A banker said it should be invested to earn interest and become an even bigger nest egg.

After a lengthy discussion, finally one older gentleman stood up slowly. He said, "Folks, I want to know who, on the day of judgment, will be willing to take this huge sum of money to the judgment seat of God and say, 'Here, Lord. Here is your money; we've saved it for you.' It's certainly not going to be me. Remember the parable of the talents."

Silence fell over the room as the respected leader

quietly sat back down with his head bowed. It was shortly decided that the money should, indeed, be invested, but in soul-reaching activities. A year later, that church was financially "on the edge," but their pews were crowded with excited new Christians, families of various nationalities seeking the one true God, and happy children riding their church buses to learn about Jesus. The old leader whose words of wisdom had caused them to invest their Master's money in souls smiled a lot. I'm sure the Master smiled too.

Parable of the Talents Matthew 25:14-30

The parable of the talents is a timeless illustration. It speaks to us today as it did to Jesus' listeners. A talent was a weight of measurement in ancient Greece, Rome, and the Middle East. It generally represented about 58 pounds. A talent of gold, or even silver, represented a large sum of money, but the dollar amount is a sideline to the story, since the talent simply represents a gift of great value.

In this story a master, getting ready to leave on a trip, called his three servants and gave to each a sum of money. Since the text says he "entrusted his property to them," the eight talents of money mentioned probably represented his total assets. He was a fair master because he did not make any one of them responsible for more than he could handle. The first servant was given five talents, the second was given two, and the third only one. It is to be understood, although it is not expressed, that each servant was well aware that the money he had was not really his own, but he was to use it to gain profit for his master.

Gift Users

According to the parable, the first two servants set to work immediately to use the master's assets to increase their value. In the time span they had, each of them doubled the amount he had been given. After a long time, the master returned and required an accounting of his money. These two servants were well rewarded.

Applying this parable allows a number of interesting inferences:

- The master obviously represents Christ himself, and the servants are his disciples (in this context) and all Christians (in the general context).

- The talents represent the potential of each Christian for service to Christ. The talents in the story were literally money, but the application is to all our resources, including money, time, spiritual gifts (see Romans 12), and opportunities.

- The master recognized that his servants were not equal in inherent abilities. So, he did not expect equal dollar results, although he did expect equal quality results—committed effort by each one.

- The amount achieved was not the basis of the rewards given. The most gifted servant was two and one-half times as productive as his two-talent co-worker. Yet, they both received exactly the same reward:

  - Each was put in charge of many things;

■ Each was invited to share his
master's happiness.

This has sometimes been regarded as a "works"
parable. That is, some believe it teaches that when
Christ returns, each of us will be rewarded on the
basis of how much he has achieved in positive results during his lifetime. It really teaches that
regardless of how much we may have achieved, we
will be judged upon faithful commitment—how well
we use what we have been given. Each of us is
responsible for trying, but the actual and eventual
results are beyond our control. In reality, this parable teaches us to use gifts of grace to express our
personal gratitude for being allowed to live on the
Master's property and use his assets. Our individual
gifts and abilities give us a natural and comfortable
way to say thank you in a productive, meaningful,
and important way.

------

*Regardless of how much
we may have achieved, we
will be judged upon faithful
commitment.*

Paul deals with this problem in 1 Corinthians 3:5-
15. He points out that in the growth of the kingdom
one person plants, another waters, but the increase
is in the hands of God. Two men may try to build
(using whatever materials are available). One man's
work survives the test of time, and he has the joy of
seeing his work bear fruit. The other man experi-
ences the tragedy of seeing his work destroyed. Still,
even though the disappointment sears his heart like
a flame, he will be saved just as the more fortunate
man will be. Each was a faithful builder. Each used

the gift of building that God had given him. Neither controlled the results of his work, but both had the desire to build.

God does not give every Christian the same gifts. In this story the master gave each of his servants different gifts. To one he gave five talents, to another he gave two, and to the third he gave one. He gives us different gifts as well. Why? To build up the body, to increase the assets of his kingdom. If and how we use these gifts is entirely up to us, but the choosing of which gift we receive is up to the Master.

Paul "worked harder than all of them" (a better translation of the Greek word *perissoteron* is "more productively"). In fact, he may have been responsible for establishing more churches than any other person in history. He admits, however, that it was not due to his own effort but to God's enabling grace. He was given unique gifts, which were enhanced by the best education, experience in two cultures, and a much-coveted citizenship (Roman). These gave him specific advantages over his fellow apostles.

Because he had given more *to* Paul, God expected more *of* Paul, and he delivered more. It does not follow that Paul's eternal reward is any greater than John's or Peter's, or Sister Lydia's who lived down the street. God still gives spiritual gifts today—not miraculous sign gifts, but motivational gifts still required to build up the body as described in Romans 12:6-8.

Gift Abusers

The servant who had been given one talent in the parable reported in last of all. He came with his rationale ready: "I knew that you are a hard man, harvesting where you have not sown and gathering where you have not scattered seed." Perhaps he thought attack was his best defense; so he tried to shift the blame to his master by calling him a crooked capitalist. He then made the excuse that because he was afraid of trying (and perhaps losing the one talent altogether), he decided to just bury the talent and keep it safe. "See, here is what belongs to you," he finished as he held out the talent to his lord.

But the master did not accept the plea, "I was afraid." He put his finger on the real motivation behind the servant's behavior. "You're wicked and lazy!" he charged him. The master did not accept the servant's accusation that he was hard. But he did grant that he expected a return on the assets he had left to the management of the servants. Actually, they were bond servants, or slaves (Greek, *dovlos*). Everything they wore, ate and used was the property of their master.

What his lord did not mention, but certainly could have, is that the servant had lived at his master's expense every day of his life. He was saved. Even so, he did not have the loyalty or appreciation to lift a finger to further his lord's interests. He failed to recognize what he had (salvation) and became ungrateful. So the sin we encounter in the lazy servant is not timidity or lack of self-confidence. It is selfishness and ingratitude. His lord reminds him that, even if he did not intend using the money himself, he could at least have passed it along to someone else (the bankers) who would have used it profitably. And today, even though a Christian may be unable to tell the Good News to someone in Shanghai personally, or feed a starving child in Haiti, he can at least help someone else who can.

Use It or Lose It!

The master then ordered that the talent be taken away from the wicked servant and given to the

servant who was most diligent. He then made this
observation: "Everyone who has will be given more,
and he will have an abundance. Whoever does not
have, even what he has will be taken from him."

Since the servant was then punished by being
thrown outside into the darkness, he lost the only
thing left to him—the privilege of living on his
master's property and sharing in its blessings. Jesus
says elsewhere that his angels "will weed out of his
kingdom everything that causes sin and all who do
evil" (Matthew 13:41).

Like the master in the parable, Christ chose to
leave his entire life's work and assets—the treasure
of salvation—in the hands of eleven very unlikely
servants. It was their responsibility to ensure that
his efforts on earth were not wasted. To that end, he
gave each of them motivational gifts to use in carrying on his work and increasing his assets—making
more Christians. Those men responded with commitment and good management of the Master's treasure, passing it on to generation after generation of
his servants.

Today that treasure rests squarely in our hands.
We must respond with equal commitment and good
management to increase the Master's assets. And he
has given each of us specific abilities and gifts to use
in that pursuit.

Romans 12:6-8 says, "We have different gifts,
according to the grace given us. If a man's gift is
prophesying, let him use it in proportion to his faith.
If it is serving, let him serve; if it is teaching, let him
teach; if it is encouraging, let him encourage; if it is
contributing to the needs of others, let him give
generously; if it is leadership, let him govern diligently; if it is showing mercy, let him do it cheer-
fully."

The point then is that *every* spiritual gift comes to

us through God's grace specifically for the purpose of increasing his assets. In other words, each one of us must learn how to use our individual gifts to reach the lost and offer them the free gift of salvation. We've tragically missed this message! We have most often limited "evangelistic" efforts to those with the gifts of speaking and teaching, rather than understanding that every gift of God is to be used for evangelism. That is, in fact, our only purpose on this earth as his servants—to increase his kingdom assets. Any other purpose is misguided and not on the Way.

There are no "housekeeping" gifts of the Spirit. There are no passive, bury-it-and-wait gifts. There are no backseat gifts, or less important gifts, or timid gifts. Every gift has its critical place and is desperately needed in our joint efforts to increase his kingdom assets. If your gift is sewing, then somehow find a way to reach out to the lost with your sewing. If your gift is music, then use your songs to touch the hearts of the lost and draw them to the Master. If your gift is parenting, then parent your children in such a way that they will become an asset to the kingdom. If your gift is making money, then learn to use the money you obtain for the spreading of the Good News and the resulting increase in the kingdom assets.

User Friendly

One Christian lady's gift was baking. She quietly went about her normal daily life baking for others. She took cakes to the neighbors. She took pies to the bereaved. She took food to the sick, to newcomers in the community, and to the needy all around her. As she went from house to house, she talked about the church she attended, and she invited the people she was helping to come with her sometime. Many times they went. And they heard the saving message of Jesus Christ. The sad part is that if you had asked this beautiful Christian if she were "evangelistic," she would have ducked her head in shame and said, "No, I'm not. I wish I were, but it's just not my gift to preach or teach." More importantly, if you had asked this faithful, committed Christian if she were saved, she would have said, "I don't know; I hope so."

There is nothing in this parable to shake the confidence of the committed Christian in the security of his salvation. There's only a warning to those who seek "cheap grace" without any commitment to fulfill God's purposes for their lives. And there is certainly no support of meritorious works as the basis of salvation. It was not the actual achievement but the motivation that determined which servants were allowed to share their Lord's happiness.

It's time for us to stop limiting our evangelistic effectiveness for the Master. We must begin to recognize and use every gift of God to increase his kingdom assets by sharing the Good News message. So remember, the Master will come back to reward "those who diligently seek him" and use their gifts he gave them for his benefit. We don't want to have to say, "Here Lord. Here's your gift; I've saved it for you." Recognizing our spiritual gifts and how we can serve the Master with them is a primary responsibility. But it's one with promise and incredible joy, happiness, and productivity.

Pearl of Wisdom:

*God has chosen you and me
to determine whether or not the
sending of his Son to earth for
the salvation of mankind will
ultimately succeed in its purpose. To that end, he has given
each one of us a special gift to
use in building faith in the
Good News of salvation that
comes through his marvelous
grace.*

Focusing Your Faith

1. What two major ideas about spiritual gifts did you glean for yourself from this chapter?

2. How would you describe the spiritual gift of grace God has given you?

3. Visualize this gift as a human being. What do you see that person doing to spread the kingdom of God?

4. Why have we shied away from allowing *all* the different gifts of grace to be used for outreach in the church and relegated evangelism to only two or three gifts (e.g., preaching and teaching)?

5. How do you feel when you are able to use your natural, God-given gift to benefit the church? How do you feel when that opportunity is unavailable or denied to you?

6. If your spiritual gift were described by a song, what song would it be? Sing the song to yourself.

7. Make a list of various ways you can begin to use your own spiritual gift to help spread the Good News.

Parable of the Rich Man and Lazarus

"There was a rich man who was dressed in purple and fine linen and lived in luxury every day. At his gate was laid a beggar named Lazarus, covered with sores and longing to eat what fell from the rich man's table. Even the dogs came and licked his sores.

"The time came when the beggar died and the angels carried him to Abraham's side. The rich man also died and was buried. In hell, where he was in torment, he looked up and saw Abraham far away, with Lazarus by his side. So he called to him, 'Father Abraham, have pity on me and send Lazarus to dip the tip of his finger in water and cool my tongue, because I am in agony in this fire.'

"But Abraham replied, 'Son, remember that in your lifetime you received your good things, while Lazarus received bad things, but now he is comforted here and you are in agony. And besides all this, between us and you a great chasm has been fixed, so that those who want to go from here to you cannot, nor can anyone cross over from there to us.'

"He answered, 'Then I beg you, father, send Lazarus to my father's house, for I have five brothers. Let him warn them, so that they will not also come to this place of torment.'

"Abraham replied, 'They have Moses and the Prophets; let them listen to them.'

" 'No, father Abraham,' he said, 'but if someone from the dead goes to them, they will repent.'

"He said to him, 'If they do not listen to Moses and the Prophets, they will not be convinced even if someone rises from the dead.' "

Luke 16:19-31

Chapter 9

Selfishness Leads *t o* Hell

D r. George W. Truett was entertained on one occasion in the home of a wealthy Texas oilman. After dinner the man took Truett up to the roof of his house and showed him huge fields of oil derricks. He said, "Dr. Truett, that's all mine. I came to this country 25 years ago penniless, and now I own everything as far as you can see in that direction."

Then he turned to the opposite direction and pointed to waving grain fields and said, "It's all mine. I own everything as far as you can see in that direction." Then he pointed to huge herds of cattle on the east and a great virgin forest on the west, saying, "It's all mine. I worked hard and saved, and today I own everything as far as you can see in every direction."

Discovery Point:

What I have is not mine to own.

He paused for the expected praise, but to his surprise it didn't come. Dr. Truett laid a loving hand on the man's shoulder, pointed upward and asked, "My friend, how much do you own in that direction?" The man dropped his head in shame and said, "I never thought of that." (Quoted in the *Western Recorder*).

Parable of the Rich Man and Lazarus Luke 16:19-31

This story, like the parable of the shrewd manager, focuses upon management of possessions. Let's begin by understanding why it was *not* intended to teach these three conclusions that have often been derived from it.

First, it does not teach that it is inherently evil to possess wealth. God blessed Solomon with such wealth that the visiting Queen of Sheba marveled that his wealth had not been described even halfway correctly. He made Abraham, Isaac, and Jacob rich men (Genesis 13:2; 26:12, 13; 30:43; 33:11). On the other hand, Jesus told the rich young ruler that to inherit eternal life he would have to give all his possessions to the poor (Luke 18:18-25). The difference is that the three patriarchs would use their wealth to serve the purposes of God, but wealth had become the young ruler's god. He chose it above eternal life.

Wealth can be a wonderful instrument for God's glory if it is used for worthwhile purposes (1 Timothy 6:17-19). Money is a great servant but a terrible master.

"Rich" and "wealthy" are relative terms. In a village of pedestrians, the owner of a bicycle is rich. In a culture of pole and mud huts, a wooden house is a palace; but in a complex of luxury dwellings that house is a hovel. Rarely will a man accept that he is

rich, because he is contrasting his million with the
fortune of a billionaire. The truth is that the average
middle-income American enjoys a standard of living
that Solomon could never have dreamed of.

*Secondly, the parable is not intended to teach that
being poor is a virtue.* If poverty is the result of
laziness, it is a harmful wrong (Proverbs 6:9, 10). A
person who gains wealth honestly and uses it wisely
is praised in the Scriptures (Proverbs 31:10-31).
There are dangers in either being very rich or very
poor (Proverbs 30:7-9). Either situation can cause a
man to separate himself from God. Paul observed
that not many people of the upper classes became
Christians (1 Corinthians 1:26). On the other hand,
two of his close friends were obviously men of wealth
(Romans 16:23 and Philemon). Jesus reported to
John the Baptist, "The good news is preached to the
poor" (Matthew 11:5). This might imply that a man's
financial worth may influence his interest in spiritual things, but Jesus may well have used the word
poor as a synonym for *humble.*

*Third, the parable is not intended to give precise
information on the world beyond death.* The text of
Luke 16:23 actually states that Lazarus was in
Abraham's "bosom." Jesus used the Pharisees' termi-
nology in speaking of future existence. The Jews
based their hope of eternal life on their being physical descendants of Abraham (Matthew 3:9). Ancient
Hebrew tombs carry the inscription, "Asleep in the
bosom of Abraham, Isaac, and Jacob." The expres-
sion is taken from their custom of a banquet host
placing the most honored guest at his immediate
right. Since they reclined diagonally at the table, the
guest's head was then near the host's chest.

Notions of an intermediate state (between physical
death and the final judgment) have resulted from
attempts to project time upon a timeless eternity.

Selfless Sharing

The real purpose of this parable is to emphasize the eternal results of really poor management of God's assets with which he has blessed us. In particular, it focuses upon an obligation to share what we have with others in greater need.

There is nothing in Jesus' description of the rich man to suggest that he had obtained his fortune illegally or dishonestly. Neither does it say that he was not respected as a person of honor in his community. There is no reason to suppose that he did not tithe or was a Sabbath breaker, or even that he did not attend the temple rituals. He probably controlled his household, studied the Scriptures and verbally acknowledged God. The rich man obviously thought he was living correctly. He certainly didn't think he would be in hell. He was surprised to be there.

Yet, he clearly made choices in life that so displeased God that he lost his hope for eternal life. Instead of admitting that he was only a manager of God's possessions, he claimed outright ownership. He spent them selfishly rather than devoting them to the needs of others. He had become so caught up in the living of life that it had blinded him to the reality of his spiritual situation.

We, like the rich man, are also so very susceptible to the subtle idolatry of materialism and selfishness. We have such incredible wealth to deal with, in comparison to the rest of this world, that it fools us—and makes fools of us. The list of life's "necessities" has lengthened greatly during the last generation or two. Labeling *wants* as *needs* is another subtle way for us to hold selfishly to what we have and keep it from use by and for others.

The parable supplies us with no resume on the

beggar. Much has been made of the fact that Jesus gave him the specific personal name Lazarus. The inference drawn by some is that the beggar was a real person, and the story is not a parable but an actual account. Lazarus was, in fact, a symbolic name which meant in Aramaic "one who is without help." That Lazarus was unable to walk is implied by his being laid at the rich man's gate. We must conclude that he lay at the gate and begged for the crumbs that fell from the rich man's table. Sadly, the rich man selfishly ignored his pitiable plight and made no effort to share with him. Jesus did not give any information about the character or religious nature of the beggar. We presume from the scene in eternity of him in the safety and comfort of Abraham that he was a good man, but in any case, the beggar is not the point of the story.

Role Reversal

Both men died and went to very different eternal abodes—the beggar to paradise and the rich man to a fiery hell. To serve the purposes of the story, the two places were within sight and earshot of each other, so that communication was possible.

The rich man's first request of Abraham was that he send Lazarus over with water to cool his tongue. Abraham pointed out that in their previous situations, their roles were reversed—Lazarus was in need of help while the rich man had lived in luxury. Abraham did not point out the irony of the current scene: the beggar who needed help from the rich man and didn't get it was now called upon to help the very person who had ignored his suffering. Another irony is that the earthly beggar now has all the riches of Abraham while the once-rich man begs for a drop of water.

A Warning from the Grave

Abraham informed the rich man that a giant chasm between paradise and hell made travel from one to the other impossible. The rich man then asked that Lazarus go back to earth and warn his five brothers so that they could avoid his hellish home. Abraham answered by telling him that his brothers were already being warned sufficiently by Moses and the prophets, just as he had been. The rich man insisted that having someone come back from the dead would make his brothers repent, but Abraham disagreed. This indicates that the rich man recognized where he had failed in his relationship to God (and man) and knew that his brothers were following the same course. Abraham's response shows that the man had violated clear instructions of Moses and the prophets, and thus the teachings of God.

Since we are not told that the rich man had done anything to break the law, then obviously he had *not* done something that the law required. We don't have to look far in the Word to find what that omission was: "Blessed is he who is kind to the needy" (Proverbs 14:21). And, "I command you to be openhanded toward your brothers and toward the poor and needy in your land" (Deuteronomy 15:11). Also, "Is not this the kind of fasting I have chosen: to loose the chains of injustice and untie the cords of the yoke, to set the oppressed free and break every yoke? Is it not to share your food with the hungry and to provide the poor wanderer with shelter—when you see the naked, to clothe him, and not to turn away from your own flesh and blood?" (Isaiah 58:6, 7). And, of course, every Jew knew how he was required to treat his neighbor: "Love your neighbor as yourself. I am the Lord" (Leviticus 19:18).

Don't Be Selfish!

This last verse implies the need for us to love ourselves. In loving ourselves we must provide for our physical, spiritual, and social needs. The verse also says we must love others as we love ourselves. Selfishness is when we meet our own personal needs at the expense of someone else. At that point, we no longer love others *as* we love ourselves; we love them *less* than ourselves. We have become self-serving rather than other-serving, just as the rich man did.

A common example of selfishness is someone who is consistently late to appointments, meetings, or even worship assemblies. That person takes for his or her own benefit time that in truth belongs to the other person, group of people, or God. They are meeting their own needs at the expense of others.

The rich man had made the fatal assumption that many make, including Christians. He had regarded the assets which the Lord had loaned him to manage as his own to use as it suited him. Those assets include our money, our time, even our love and kindness. If we are unfaithful in our use of worldly wealth, God will not give us true riches (Luke 16:11). If we are "faithful over a few things" (earthly possessions) we will be given "many things" (heaven's riches).

Like the rich man, we can be "faithful members" of the Lord's body. We can give to support the church budget, attend church assemblies, not drink or smoke or lie or sleep around. Still, we may not be dealing with the reality of selfishness that controls our attitudes and actions toward others.

It's true that we cannot share enough of our assets to earn our way to heaven, but according to this parable of Jesus, if we are *not* sharing, we are not going to heaven.

When we look into the eyes of a hungry man, we are staring into the gaunt face of Jesus Christ himself: "For I was hungry and you gave me nothing to eat. . . . I tell you the truth, whatever you did not do for one of the least of these, you did not do for me" (Matthew 25:42-45).

•————————————————————————————————————•

It is ironic that a story intended to emphasize the critical and eternal importance of stewardship in this life has often been the principal focus of curiosity about the next life. Some say the parable is describing an intermediate state between death and the judgment where disembodied spirits are awaiting the resurrection of their bodies and the succeeding universal judgment. That position is confronted by two considerable difficulties:

1. Lazarus and the rich man were not disembodied spirits. The rich man had a tongue and Lazarus had a finger (Luke 16:24).

2. They were hardly awaiting a judgment, since they clearly had already been judged and consigned to different fates on the basis of that judgment.

To try to make specific application of the circumstantial parameters of a parable is to go beyond its terms of reference, which is to teach principles that relate to becoming what God wants us to be. The only human being in the Scriptures (unless we use John as having been literally present in heaven during the Revelation) to be allowed to view the celestial paradise and return to earth was the apostle Paul (2 Corinthians 12:2-4). He was unable to tell what he saw and heard. They were "inexpressible things." The NIV translates: "things that man is not permitted to tell," but the Greek construction ouk exon can be translated "impossible" as well as "impermissible," and that seems to be the correct sense here. Since man can only describe anything unknown by comparison to things already known or experienced, no language is adequate to express nor any human mind able to visualize life in another dimension. What can be clearly understood is that use of our opportunities here and now determine where we will spend eternity, and that once earthly life is over it is too late for repentance to affect that destiny.

Pearl of Wisdom:

Selfishness demonstrates a misunderstanding about the true ownership of my possessions here on earth. They are not mine to own; they are only on loan to manage for the Master.

Focusing Your Faith

1. What feelings motivate us to be selfish and money grabbing?

2. Make a list of ways you see yourself being selfish.

3. Selfishness is sly and deceptive. How does selfishness deceive you most often?

4. What do think Satan has whispered in your ear recently to tempt you toward selfishness?

5. Why do sharing with others and sacrificial giving add *so much* joy to life?

6. Suppose you were able to totally eliminate any form of selfishness from your life, and you became completely self*less*. What would your life become?

7. With what, other than money, are you most selfish? How can that be overcome?

Parable of the Soils

*Then he told them many things in parables, saying:
"A farmer went out to sow his seed. As he was scattering
the seed, some fell along the path, and the birds came and
ate it up. Some fell on rocky places, where it did not have
much soil. It sprang up quickly, because the soil was
shallow. But when the sun came up, the plants were
scorched, and they withered because they had no root.
Other seed fell among thorns, which grew up and choked
the plants. Still other seed fell on good soil, where it
produced a crop—a hundred, sixty or thirty times what
was sown. He who has ears, let him hear."*

*"Listen then to what the parable of the sower means:
When anyone hears the message about the kingdom and
does not understand it, the evil one comes and snatches
away what was sown in his heart. This is the seed sown
along the path. The one who received the seed that fell on
rocky places is the man who hears the word and at once
receives it with joy. But since he has no root, he lasts only
a short time. When trouble or persecution comes because
of the word, he quickly falls away. The one who received
the seed that fell among the thorns is the man who hears
the word, but the worries of this life and the deceitfulness
of wealth choke it, making it unfruitful. But the one who
received the seed that fell on good soil is the man who
hears the word and understands it. He produces a crop,
yielding a hundred, sixty or thirty times what was sown."*

Matthew 13:3-9, 18-23

Chapter 10

Mar. 24 '94

We Are
a Sowing
People

Discovery Point:

*Even I can share
my faith.*

In England in the 1860s a Manchester physician was awakened in the middle of a cold, rainy night. It was one of the Welsh coal miners from the rows of small cottages that sprawled near the distant coal main. The man's wife was in labor, and her strength was ebbing fast. The doctor was needed urgently to save the lives of both mother and infant.

The doctor was tired and frustrated by overwork, and the prospect of walking through the mud on that cold stormy night was appalling. His thoughts were, "Why don't I make an excuse? What difference would it make whether the world had one more miserable coal miner's brat?" But, of course, he went in spite of his reluctance. The coal miner's "brat" who was delivered that night was David Lloyd

George, who grew up to be one of the greatest prime ministers Great Britain ever had.

You see, the doctor's calling was to deliver babies, not to choose which babies to deliver. And so is our calling as sharers of faith.

Soils and Sowing

First-century Palestine's economy was mainly based on farming. The lifestyle of the people was centered around the planting-and-harvesting cycle. In good seasons, when the early and latter rains fell normally, rich harvests were reaped from fertile areas like the Plain of Esdraelon in Galilee. Other areas were less favored and often rocky and the peasants were really subsistence farmers. They ate well when their crops flourished and suffered great poverty when the harvest failed due to drought, locusts, or other threats to their precarious lives.

Their chief crops were grain—wheat in a few higher rainfall areas, but small patches of barley throughout most of the country. We know from biblical references (Judges 7:13; John 6:9; Revelation 6:6) that the average man's staple diet was coarse barley bread. Bread was the staff which supported all life (Leviticus 26:26). So, when Jesus talked about sowing and reaping, he was touching a very sensitive chord in the hearts of his hearers.

Parable of the Soils Matthew 13:3-9, 18-23

Perhaps the best known parable about sowing is recorded in Matthew. Jesus' story described a farmer who planted his entire field, which contained four different types of soil. Taking a handful of seeds from a pouch slung over his shoulder, the farmer made a sweeping movement of his arm and scattered seeds as evenly as he could in a wide arc. He did not avoid those patches of ground that he suspected would not produce grain; he planted the whole field.

Some of the soil repelled the seeds because it was simply too hard for seeds to penetrate. Some of the soil was rocky, and it only allowed the seeds to fit in between the rocks and grow temporarily. The third soil was infested with stickers and thorny weeds, which choked out the good seeds the farmer sowed. But the fourth soil was rich and fertile—the seeds came up and produced beautiful grain in abundance.

The Planter's Job

The planter in this story knew his job; it was to plant. His goal was to scatter the good seeds over the entire field. That's all. When the seeds had been planted, his job was done as a planter.

The planter represents a sharer of faith today, which all Christians have been instructed to be. Our job is to share our faith, using whatever gift or ability God has given us. The farmer farmed; so, that's how he planted. We must plant our faith in the natural way God has given us, whether through our business, our art, our conversation, or some other gift.

Sharing our faith is not just for preachers and teachers. In Acts 2:41-47 it's clear that the church multiplied to several thousand rapidly, but there were only twelve preachers in the beginning. The primary growth came from the faith sharing done by the Christians in those hundreds of house churches as they enjoyed the favor of all the people (verse 47). By meeting the needs of people inside and outside their small groups, they were seen by the community as loving and caring. By their very nature of striving to be Christlike, they planted the golden seeds of the Word of life. And God gave the increase.

Unfortunately, we have often mistakenly expanded the planter's job description. We have insisted that he not only plant, but that he water, hoe, deweed, reseed, and harvest the crop, too. Likewise, we have expected Christians—*all* Christians, regardless of their talents from God—to be full-service evangelists. We expect them not only to share their faith, naturally, but also to teach, encourage, convict, and convert each person with whom they have shared their faith. Nothing could be more counterproductive in the church.

To Each His Own

The Scriptures are plain in teaching that God gave each Christian a particular gift to use in spreading his kingdom. He did not give all Christians all gifts. Why? Consider this: If each Christian had all gifts, we would not need each other at all; we'd each be self-sufficient. Also, unity in the body of Christ would be impossible; competition would be the name of the game.

No, as always, God is all-wise. He draws us together as a body by giving each part of the body a different and necessary function. "But to each one of us grace has been given as Christ apportioned it. . . . It was he who gave some to be apostles, some to be prophets, some to be evangelists, and some to be pastors and teachers, to prepare God's people for works of service, so that the body of Christ may be built up until we all reach unity in the faith and in the knowledge of the Son of God and become mature, attaining to the whole measure of the fullness of Christ" (Ephesians 4:7, 11-13). In other words, to ever reach maturity in Christ, we have to learn to need each other and respect each other's individual gift of grace. Only then can the entire cycle of planting, watering, tending, and harvesting work effectively.

We are faith sharers every one, using our own natural gifts of grace from Christ. And together we can bring in God's crop, which is now ready to harvest. As Paul said in 1 Corinthians 3:6, "I planted the seed [he was a planter!], Apollos watered it [using his gift of grace], but God made it grow." It's a team effort, not some macho-Christian heroic run around the end, and God is the quarterback.

Most of us who are not preachers probably carry significant guilt around with us over ignoring the Great Commission. Our unstated question might be, "Why did God hang such a requirement on me? I thought we were saved by grace, but here seems to be something I have to *do*. And *doing* sounds like works salvation."

> *If each Christian had all gifts, we would not need each other at all.*

As in all God's commandments, though, when this one is carried out, it's for our own benefit and blessing. God promises us blessings that are not available to us until we experience sharing our faith with others. Philemon 6 says a full understanding of everything we have in Christ Jesus is only available to those who are actively sharing their faith. First Corinthians 9:22 says that Paul spent his entire life sharing his faith so that he might share in its blessings. We know from Ephesians 2:8, 9 that Paul knew he could not earn his salvation; so, he must be talking about the full understanding of what we have in Christ Jesus we noted above.

There is an incredible joy and Godlikeness that accompanies a Christian who is fulfilling his role as a faith sharer (planter). He becomes a part of the creative nature of God himself. He does good deeds for others out of gratitude to God for his own salvation, not in order to earn his salvation. He helps others because of his God-instructed agape love for them.

The blessing? He becomes more like God. He feels great joy in knowing that he is carrying out his special assignment from God. He receives love and appreciation from the people he helps. He gains a fuller understanding of everything that he has in Christ Jesus. That is a glimpse of God. That is the greatest blessing available to man.

Here are three other general inferences we may draw from this parable:

1. *The sower cannot expect universal acceptance of his message because human hearts are different,* just as the farmer knows that all soils are not equally productive. As much as the Christian would like for every hearer of his message to be eagerly responsive, it is unrealistic to expect it. It won't happen, even under the most favorable of circumstances.

2. *The sower's job is to sow the entire field without avoiding stony patches or areas where "stickers" may grow.* Every kind of soil must be given an opportunity to produce something. Christians do not have the right to judge who is worthy or unworthy to receive the gospel, but we must make every effort to see that it is shared with all mankind, just as the Manchester physician gave care to all who needed it, not just babies with great promise.

3. *The sower was abundantly successful in his efforts once he had planted the entire field.* He did his job as a planter. The seeds had been scattered everywhere, and it would naturally come up where the soil was fertile. God would make it grow.

Paul says it well in Galatians 6:9: "Let us not

become weary in doing good, for at the proper time we will reap a harvest if we do not give up." Don't quit planting! Continue to share the faith, and souls will be won to Christ—it is inevitable, because God will make it grow where hearts are open and fertile.

Faith or Failure?

We think of Jesus as the most successful of teachers, yet after three and one-half years of constant and strenuous preaching, he had only a 120 followers to show for it. That doesn't seem like many. But those 120 followers started an evangelistic movement that spread around the world and continues even today through you and me—if we are sharing our faith.

Paul preached brilliantly at Athens (Acts 17). Perhaps there is no better example of an eloquent sermon than the one he preached on Mars Hill, but he was ridiculed for his efforts. Luke dismisses the Athens campaign as a failure with his brief paragraph: "A few men became followers of Paul and believed. Among them was Dionysius, a member of the Areopagus, also a woman named Damaris, and a number of others. After this, Paul left Athens and went to Corinth."

History, however, assigns a victorious value to Paul's meeting at Athens. In the first quarter of the second century, the young church was pitted against the might of Rome and its state religion. Two of the most brilliant defenders of the Christian faith, Athenagoras and Aristides, came out of that unpromising Athenian congregation. Paul's planting was successful, and God had given the increase, just as he promised.

God's promise has not changed. If we share our faith in him today, in whatever natural way he has given us to use, he will still give the increase, and

"the Lord is not slow in keeping his promises"
(2 Peter 3:9). We are often just slow in claiming
them.

Parable of Wheat and Weeds Matthew 13:24-30, 36-43

In the second sowing parable, the application has
a slightly different twist. Instead of representing the
word of the kingdom, the seeds now stand for Christians themselves—the means have become the
results.

A man (the owner) planted grain in his field.
Because his servants are mentioned later, we may
infer that he had his servants do the planting. The
seeds were good, and in due time they sprouted.
When his workers went to check on the growing
crop, they were dismayed to find that weeds (actually, *darnel* or "false wheat") were growing among
the stalks of grain. The owner knew immediately
that his enemy had crept into the field at night and
planted the false wheat. The enemy knew that the
darnel would be almost impossible to remove. Darnel was difficult to identify and practically impossible to remove since their roots so entwined with
the real wheat roots.

His servants suggested they pull out the false
wheat, but this idea was not helpful. The owner
pointed out that it would be impossible to pull out
the darnel without also uprooting the grain. He told
his workers to leave the weeds alone until the crop
was ready. Then the harvesters could separate the
wheat from the false wheat without causing damage.

Darnel, unlike the thorny weeds of the earlier
parable, did not completely choke out the barley or
wheat. Although it was undesirable because it
competed for the soil's nourishment and moisture,
the good grain would still survive and produce.

Parable of the Wheat and Weeds

Jesus told them another parable: "The kingdom of heaven is like a man who sowed good seed in his field. But while everyone was sleeping, his enemy came and sowed weeds among the wheat, and went away. When the wheat sprouted and formed heads, then the weeds also appeared.

"The owner's servants came to him and said, 'Sir, didn't you sow good seed in your field? Where then did the weeds come from?'

" 'An enemy did this,' replied.

"The servants asked him, 'Do you want us to go and pull them up?'

" 'No,' he answered, 'because while you are pulling the weeds, you may root up the wheat with them. Let both grow together until the harvest. At that time I will tell the harvesters: First collect the weeds and tie them in bundles to be burned; then gather the wheat and bring it into my barn.' "

Then he left the crowd and went into the house. His disciples came to him and said, "Explain to us the parable of the weeds in the field."

He answered, "The one who sowed the good seed is the Son of Man. The field is the world, and the good seed stands for the sons of the kingdom. The weeds are the sons of the evil one, and the enemy who sows them is the devil. The harvest is the end of the age, and the harvesters are angels.

"As the weeds are pulled up and burned in the fire, so it will be at the end of the age. The Son of Man will send out his angels, and they will weed out of his kingdom everything that causes sin and all who do evil. They will throw them into the fiery furnace, where there will be weeping and gnashing of teeth. Then the righteous will shine like the sun in the kingdom of their Father. He who has ears, let him hear."

Matthew 13:24-30, 36-43

Parable of the Growing Seed

He also said, "This is what the kingdom of God is like. A man scatters seed on the ground. Night and day, whether he sleeps or gets up, the seed sprouts and grows, though he does not know how. All by itself the soil produces grain—first the stalk, then the head, then the full kernel in the head. As soon as the grain is ripe, he puts the sickle to it, because the harvest has come."

Mark 4:26-29

Pulling out the darnel would uproot much of the grain; so, that was not really an option.

What, then, is the application of this parable? Half-hearted Christians would not be represented by the darnel, since false wheat is not wheat at all; it only appears to be. A true parable would suggest that there are members in our fellowship who have not actually been converted to Christ. To put it another way, they are accepted as members of the congregation, but they are not truly in Christ's spiritual body, the church. They wear the guise of Christians, but they do not bear any fruit. They are "darnel Christians," in effect.

How can we get rid of these impostors? Jesus says we can't; we are not even to try lest we uproot and do terrible damage to the church. "Darnel Christians" are subject to the same church discipline as are true Christians. They are to receive no special treatment. It simply means that God did not give us the responsibility for passing judgment on who does or does not belong to him.

In one important area the darnel does not correspond to the unconverted "Christian." The darnel does not have the potential to become wheat. It is just what it is and can never become something else. People, on the other hand, can change their relationship to God anytime they submit to the will of Christ. That is a very important reason for leaving uncommitted members in the fellowship. They can change, and they are more likely to change for the better in a true Christian environment than in the world.

Parable of the Growing Seed Mark 4:26-29

Another parable of sowing is that of the seed growing secretly. A man scatters good seed on the soil. He then goes about his ordinary life: sleeping, eating, working, etc. While he is busy at other things, the combination of seed and soil, quite independent of the man himself, go about their assigned roles of producing a crop until the harvest is ready.

The principal lesson seems to be abundantly clear: We should perform our assigned job—sharing our faith—and leave the process of growth to God. By assuming direct responsibility for the results, we take on a burden we cannot carry and were never meant to carry.

The man could have spent his nights watching over the field instead of sleeping, but the results would not have been influenced by his depriving himself of rest. He could have worried himself to distraction over whether the seeds would sprout, whether the rain would come, or whether the locusts would devour the crop. The outcome would still have been the same.

Let God Be God

Jesus' message is this: Let God be God, and trust him to take care of things you cannot control. The fact is, *we* cannot convert anybody; only the Word of God can convict and convert the lost. We cannot save anybody; only God himself can save the lost with his merciful grace. The only possible thing we can do is expose others to the Word to help a lost person develop his own faith, because faith comes from hearing the Word of God (Romans 10:17). When we have shared the basis for our faith, we have done our job. God will do the rest. We have succeeded in our God-given task, whether the person responds to God or not.

This parable is written to encourage us when we are despondent at the apparent lack of results from our efforts to spread the kingdom and when we may

be tempted to give up altogether. Although the
parable covers only four short verses, it contains
valuable lessons.

It is a certain and sure process. God's word does
not return to him empty (Isaiah 55:11). As Jesus
points out in the parable of the soils, the gospel will
fall upon indifferent and careless ears. But it will
certainly fall upon earnest and sincere ears as well.
Not every seed will germinate, but if the planting is
done earnestly and carefully, enough will grow to
produce a harvest. It is God who gives the increase
(1 Corinthians 3:6), so we do not have to make
despairing forecasts of a fruitless outcome. Our job is
faithfulness in sharing the Word. The results are in
the hands of God.

It is a divine process. We do not have to understand how the growth is going to be achieved in
order to do our job of planting. Through the Word,
the Spirit will convict the world of sin, righteousness, and judgment (John 16:8-11). The Word is
designed by God to do just that; so we do not need to
worry about whether or not it is going to work
effectively.

A doctor may prescribe an antibiotic for a patient,
but whether or not it is effective is out of his hands.
The therapeutic power is in the drug itself. He
cannot enhance it by crossing his fingers, giving a
donation to charity, or sitting up all night worrying.
Its actual success depends on the patient's freewill
choice to swallow the medicine or not. And a soul
must decide for himself whether he will internalize
God's Word and, thus, be healed from his spiritual
sickness.

It is a gradual process. The farmer, eager to
realize a profit from his harvest, goes through a
fever of impatience at the slow pace at which the
sprouting seed grows into mature corn. In the same

way, many parents do great harm to their children by pushing them into sophisticated endeavors for which they are not yet ready, thereby short-circuiting their normal development. A preacher endures agonies of frustration waiting for his first converts, and then he undergoes the long anxious vigil until they grow into useful Christians. Yet, this will happen eventually, if he doesn't become too impatient and interfere with the process by giving the newborns "meat" before they have had their "milk." This is a period which tries his faith in God's method.

Jesus' teaching in this parable just has to be true. The church is growing throughout the world, but I cannot possibly see how. We are so fickle, haphazard, selfish, and short-sighted in our approach to world evangelism that any human enterprise operated along the same lines would be doomed to failure. Yet, the kingdom spreads. Considering what kind of farmhands the Lord has to depend upon, the process itself has to be divine, or Christianity would have been extinct ages ago. Instead, hearts are still won to Christ. Faith is still shared. And souls are still eternally redeemed. All praise, glory, and honor to the God of heaven who alone can cause the increase by using pitiful-but-sincere planters such as we.

> ## Pearl of Wisdom:
>
> *God has a very special blessing available only to planters (faith sharers), who know they were created to plant and use their natural spiritual gifts and talents in that task. They are the only ones who ever gain a "full understanding of every good thing we have in Christ."*

Focusing Your Faith

1. Why is God's divine plan for each Christian to use his individual, God-appointed gift to "plant the seed" superior to our usual practice of evangelizing in the church today?

2. What feelings do you experience when you know you have effectively planted a small seed of God?

3. What do you think would happen in the church if we truly believed and practiced this truth about evangelizing that was in the chapter: "It's a team effort, not some macho-Christian heroic run around the end, and God is the quarterback"?

4. "Evangelism is any word or act that moves another person even slightly closer to God." With this definition in mind, what do others at church see you doing that would be defined as evangelism? At work? In recreational activities?

5. How do we often deal with "darnel Christians" differently than the way taught in this parable?

6. Do you hear Jesus laughing or crying at the way you most often live this parable? Why?

7. Make a list of *new* ways you can use your spiritual gift/talent to "evangelize" (see number 4 above).

Parable of the Mustard Seed and Yeast

He told them another parable: "The kingdom of heaven is like a mustard seed, which a man took and planted in his field. Though it is the smallest of all your seeds, yet when it grows, it is the largest of garden plants and becomes a tree, so that the birds of the air come and perch in its branches."

He told them still another parable: "The kingdom of heaven is like yeast that a woman took and mixed into a large amount of flour until it worked all through the dough."

Matthew 13:31-33

Chapter 11

Why Don't You Grow Up?

At the beginning of this century a Christian stonemason from New Zealand traveled up the African continent from Cape Town. He was on a commission from the British South Africa Company to erect a stone base for

Discovery Point:

God turns my small beginnings into great endings.

a statue of David Livingstone at the Victoria Falls. He established the small masonry yard at the frontier town of Bulowayo in the crown colony of Southern Rhodesia. The man was John Sheriff—a Christian by vocation and a mason by occupation, and the first preacher of the gospel in British Central Africa.

Among the native helpers whom Sheriff employed were three young men who were destined to change the spiritual face of the African subcontinent: Peter Masia from Northern Rhodesia; Jack Mzirwa from Mashonaland in Southern Rhodesia; and George

Khosa, a Mozambique orphan who had escaped a massacre in his home country at the age of six and had grown up in the Union of South Africa. An unseen force drew this remarkable trio of men to the little stoneyard in Bulawayo.

One night John Sheriff saw a light still burning in the young men's hut late in the night and went to investigate. As he drew near he could hear that they were laboriously sounding out words from the Bible. He knocked at their door, and upon being invited to enter, he asked if they would like for him to start reading classes for them. They eagerly agreed, and so the four men began studies that resulted in the conversion of the three black youths.

These men were filled with zeal to share their new-found treasure with their own people. Peter Masia went back across the Zambezi River to the Livingstone district in what is now Zambia. After terrible hardships and persecution, he established a church on a site that later became Sinde Mission, the beginning of the great Zambian work. Jack Mzirwa returned to the eastern highlands of Southern Rhodesia. His powerful preaching began the first of many churches in that area where Nhowe mission would some day be built. And George, the orphan from Mozambique, traveled south to Johannesburg to preach among the thousands of his fellow Shangaan tribesmen who worked in the South African gold mines. Many of those whom he converted returned to establish churches in their home villages in Mozambique.

John Sheriff always called George Khosa his "mustard seed." But the real mustard seed was John Sheriff himself, a dedicated Christian. With a hammer in one hand and a Bible in the other, he started the growth process which eventually led to thousands of churches in central and southern Africa today.

Mustard Seed and Yeast Matthew 13:31-33

Jesus was the master communicator because he drew his lesson principles from the ordinary things of people's everyday lives. One of the areas of life that every human being is concerned with is his diet. Only a very small part of the earth's population in any age has much choice about what or how much they eat. Just surviving is their main concern, so any reference to food is of interest.

The great Caesars, for instance, averted the threat from Roman mobs by distributing bread at state expense. And, Marie Antoinette paid with her head for making light of the hunger of the women of Paris. But bread is no laughing matter to starving people. It's a matter of life and death. In our affluent society, we often make jokes about putting someone on a ration of bread and water for misbehaving, knowing full well that even the prisoners in our jails eat far above that level.

Palestine in the days of Jesus was very much what twenty-first century Americans would call "a third world country." Only wealthy people could afford a diet heavy in protein, especially red meats. Except in the case of whole burnt offerings, a Jew got most of the flesh from animals he sacrificed, after the priests had taken their share.

Even so, many of the poor had to substitute turtle doves (pigeons) as sacrifices for the animals they could not afford. Apart from the temple rituals, animals were slaughtered for very special social occasions. Dried fish were, and still are in most of the East and Africa, a main source of protein, but they did not make up the bulk of a meal. This is well illustrated in John 6 where the food carried by a small boy consisted of five barley loaves and two small fish. Vegetables such as lentils, chicory, endive, onions, garlic, and mustard provided the "sauce" that made their coarse bread palatable. Mustard and bread still go hand in hand today, even in our own society, as we use mustard to spice up sandwiches and other foods. And we still depend on bread as a dietary staple.

Mustard was valued for both its leaves and its pungent seed. It was thought remarkable because of the smallness of the seed compared to the large size of its mature plant, which could grow several feet high. Jesus' observation that the seed is "smaller than all the seeds" must be understood contextually, rather than as an absolute. The NIV translates his statement this way: "Though it is the smallest of all your seeds." The *your* is not in the original language, but that is clearly the sense of the passage. Otherwise, a skeptic might point out that a eucalyptus seed is actually much smaller than a mustard seed, yet produces a 300-foot-high tree.

Personal Growth

The extreme contrast between the seed from which a mustard plant sprouts and the impressive size of the full-grown bush gives great force to Jesus' parable. The growth shown by the mustard seed has a real application to the spiritual growth of a Christian. Newborn Christians, like newborn human infants, do not have the depth of knowledge and experience to make them as effective workers as the more mature members. They, like a sprouted mustard seed, need care and cultivation. Later, as they increase in spiritual stamina and size, they will be able to withstand the weeds of life and occasional periods of drought. But during their initial growth, they are vulnerable to the arrows of the devil, unless they are loved and protected by other Christians who are older in the faith.

In the Arctic regions, the young of two species of grazing animals—the caribou and the musk ox—are easy prey for packs of Arctic wolves if left unprotected. Since there are no forests in which they can hide, their survival depends entirely upon the protection of the adult animals of their species. The adult musk oxen form a circle with their calves inside. A wolf does not stupidly throw himself against the sharp horns facing him.

The caribou not only form a protective circle around their young, but the ring of adult animals constantly race around the closely packed calves so that the attackers must breech a "circle saw" of antlers and flailing hooves. In a less dramatic but equally real way, mature Christians must form a protective circle around those "little ones" in the faith who cannot survive the battles of life without help.

To grow to adults in their spiritual lives, new Christians must be given food that will help them develop. As Peter points out in 1 Peter 2:2, newborn babes require pure milk for their growth (i.e. simple, faith-building teaching that will strengthen and not overwhelm them). There comes a time, though, when growth is stopped if they do not go on to more mature understanding (see Hebrews 6:1-3). Paul was disappointed that the Corinthian Christians had not grown up in the things of Christ but were still in the milk stage of development and could not digest solid spiritual food (1 Corinthians 3:2).

The church of God is a corporate support system for helping those who are young in the faith to grow into spiritual maturity in a loving and caring family. Christ commissioned apostles and prophets to begin the process of building up the spiritual newborns until they find a place of meaningful service in the body (Ephesians 4:11-13). They passed on this responsibility to evangelists, teachers, and pastors. The elders of the church have a special commission to shepherd the flock. Teachers also have a serious responsibility (James 3:1), but every mature, or maturing, Christian has a God-given charge to strengthen those who are not as far along the spiritual road as themselves (1 Thessalonians 5:14). The process of growth is not complete until the seedling has become a sturdy, fruit-bearing plant itself and realizes the purpose that was inherent in the seed when it was planted. (See Colossians 2:6, 7.)

Sourdough Christians

The parable of the leaven immediately follows the mustard seed lesson (Matthew 13:33). Although expressed in a single verse, it contains a wealth of meaning. The NIV translation "yeast" might suggest to us a small, foil-wrapped square bought in a supermarket and containing a cream cheeselike substance used to make homemade bread or dinner rolls.

Our great-grandmothers would have had a different image from the parable: a small container on the back of the kitchen range containing a piece of dough rescued from a loaf of bread before it was baked, bubbling in a nutrient solution of potato water or a flour mixture. This "starter," as it was called, became the leavening agent for future batches of bread.

Prospectors of the Old West were often called "sourdoughs" because a stoppered bottle of such a solution was most always found in the supplies their pack donkeys carried. When a little of the potent sourdough was mixed with flour, water, and salt, it produced a bread loaf the prospector baked over the open fire in his iron pot.

Bread was, and is, the basic diet in Palestine and the whole Middle East. Archaeologists, digging in the ruins of the cities of ancient Israel, have uncovered hundreds of clay ovens. Some were permanent ovens intended for commercial use; others were little more than a bowl, which was placed over the pan of dough and covered with coals. Their product was the staple food of both rich and poor. The difference was the type of flour used to make the loaf—wheat if you were well-off, barley if you weren't. Then, as now in much of the world, to "break bread" meant to eat a meal. Bread was so nearly their total diet that "bread" equated with "food." "Rice" is used in a similar way in parts of Asia today where it is the principal grain. When a Chinese person asks, "Have you eaten rice?" he is not only asking whether you are eating regularly, but about your general well-being.

The imagery of mixing a small lump of sourdough into moistened flour differs in one way from the figure of a mustard seed. With the mustard, the seed itself grows into a large plant. The lump of yeast or sourdough, though, permeates all the surrounding dough. The mustard seed best fits the personal growth of a Christian through the Word. The yeast suggests how a Christian's life influences others—in other words, lifestyle evangelism.

Jesus compares his followers to a city set on a hill and a lamp put on a stand. He is referring to the influence of the Christian's life, as shown by this application: "In the same way, let your light shine before men, that they may see your good deeds and praise your Father in heaven" (Matthew 5:16). Often people whose ears seem to be closed to the Godlike Christ they envision from the spoken gospel respond to the humanlike Christ they see living in Christians they know.

For example, Peter gives this advice to Christian wives who are trying without success to convert their unbelieving husbands: "They may be won over without words by the behavior of their wives, when they see the purity and reverence of your lives" (1 Peter 3:1, 2).

The early Christians exerted a powerful influence in the pagan world of the Roman Empire. One heathen critic complained that the new religion was not being spread by proper preachers at all but "by a community of cobblers and tailors." A Roman emperor exclaimed in despair, "We Romans help nobody but ourselves. The Jews will help other Jews. But these Christians will help everybody, including Romans." When we recapture the uniqueness of the early church, perhaps once again men will exclaim, "These people have turned the world upside down."

Set Aside for Growth

The mustard seed and the yeast both represent the kingdom of God. They show God's ruling and reigning activity in the lives of men today. From something very small and seemingly insignificant, such as a mustard seed or a bit of sourdough (budding faith), the whole Christian is impacted and changed during the maturing process. And, yet, it doesn't happen all at once. In making bread, the sourdough is mixed in, then the bread is set aside to rise for several hours. In the same way, the Word of God enters a person's heart where it matures slowly through the years until that person becomes more like Christ himself—the Bread of Life.

A good example of this process is Saul, who retreated to Arabia to study and learn for some three years soon after the words of Jesus penetrated his heart and he became a Christian. (See Galatians 1:15-24.) When he returned, he was a powerful witness for Christ. His faith had budded, blossomed, and was ready to bear fruit.

In the same way, new Christians need a time of personal faith building and maturing before they are thrown into the demanding roles of mature Christians. They need to be "set aside" like the newly blended bread so they can rise to the challenge of being effective servants of the Lord. So often we rush them into service for our own benefit—because we are tired of teaching or driving the bus or working with the teenagers. We may use them for an "out" for us or some other weary Christian. That's often a mistake, because new Christians are not equipped yet to meet the demands of others, and the result is that the new Christians become overloaded and discouraged. Many times they even leave the fellowship, convinced that they cannot "keep up" with the rest of us or survive the strains the extra duties place on their own lives and the lives of their families.

Instead, we need to view new Christians as young children. We need to nurture and teach them and help them learn how to walk and talk. We need to feed them the Word in small bites that they can handle and help them grow up in Christ. Does it take a lot of effort on our part? Yes. Few tasks can be more demanding than helping a new Christian mature. And, yet, the reward of watching them grow is exhilarating.

Mix Well

Whether or not the seed is allowed to grow or the yeast is allowed to permeate our lives is in our control. We either mix the sourdough solution (God's Word) into our lives, or we keep it bottled up in a separate place where it is ineffective for us. God's kingdom within us must be free to penetrate all the vital parts of our lives—our intellectual lives, our professional lives, our social, recreational, and emotional lives. Then, little by little, the leaven can even out our lives and give us balance and maturity.

Bread for a Hungry World

Peter said this same thing in another way in 2 Peter 1:3-11 when he said that we need to have faith, goodness, knowledge, self-control, perseverance, godliness, brotherly kindness, and love in increasing measure. It's not enough to have a little faith and leave it at that. We must constantly be working to increase our faith. The same is true with each of these areas of life. That boils down to letting God's Word do its work in our hearts, minds, and actions. The result is that as our faith, goodness, knowledge, self-control, perseverance, godliness, brotherly kindness, and love increase, we will become more and more like God himself, whose traits these are. And the next undeniable occurrence is that the people around us will see it and be drawn to the Savior within us. We will become the Bread of Life to the starving people we touch every day.

Here again, as we've mentioned in connection with other parables, giving people the Bread of Life is a natural thing. It's the result of living a life in tune with the song of God. It's not a forced, unnatural Bible-banging attempt to make people accept the truth whether they want it or not. It's a naturally magnetic attraction of people who are seeking the truth toward the heavenly traits of God that are visible in your life. It's evangelizing just by living your life in accord with God's Word. That alone will make you so unusual and unique that others cannot help but be drawn to you and your life style. They will be drawn to your happiness and joy. They will be drawn to your ability to cope with the disasters of life with a smile and radiating hope. They will be drawn to your self-confidence that comes from your knowledge that God himself lives within you. They will be drawn to his kindness and mercy and love, which they experience through your kindness and mercy and love. And the little seed of faith you help them plant within their hearts will grow into hearty, mature trees of joy and salvation.

Pearl of Wisdom:

God can turn small beginnings into great endings. Seeds of faith can become towering trees of spiritual strength and leadership.

Focusing Your Faith

1. When you see a mature Christian, what makes you identify him or her as mature?

2. How can mature Christians form a "circle saw" of protection around new Christians, as the caribou do around their young?

3. What does "sourdough Christian" mean to you?

4. Sing a song to yourself (or someone else) that
    expresses your own desire to "grow up" in your
    spiritual life as a mustard seed grows into a tree.

5. What would you become if you truly allowed
    God's kingdom within you to penetrate all these
    vital areas: your intellectual life, your profes-
    sional life, your social life, your recreational life,
    and your emotional life?

6. Paul took a "time out" of three years in his life
    after he became a new Christian. Why would
    doing that be important to Christians today?

7. How have your feelings changed as you have
    matured in your spiritual life?

Parable of the Ten Virgins

"At that time the kingdom of heaven will be like ten virgins who took their lamps and went out to meet the bridegroom. Five of them were foolish and five were wise. The foolish ones took their lamps but did not take any oil with them. The wise, however, took oil in jars along with their lamps. The bridegroom was a long time in coming, and they all became drowsy and fell asleep.

"At midnight the cry rang out: 'Here's the bridegroom! Come out to meet him!'

"Then all the virgins woke up and trimmed their lamps. The foolish ones said to the wise, 'Give us some of your oil; our lamps are going out.'

" 'No,' they replied, 'there may not be enough for both us and you. Instead, go to those who sell oil and buy some for yourselves.'

"But while they were on their way to buy the oil, the bridegroom arrived. The virgins who were ready went in with him to the wedding banquet. And the door was shut.

"Later the others also came. 'Sir! Sir!' they said. 'Open the door for us!'

"But he replied, 'I tell you the truth, I don't know you.'

"Therefore keep watch, because you do not know the day or the hour."

Matthew 25:1-13

Parable of the Watchful Servants

"No one knows about that day or hour, not even the angels in heaven, nor the Son, but only the Father. Be on guard! Be alert! You do not know when that time will come. It's like a man going away: He leaves his house and puts his servants in charge, each with his assigned task, and tells the one at the door to keep watch.

"Therefore keep watch because you do not know when the owner of the house will come back—whether in the evening, or at midnight, or when the rooster crows, or at dawn. If he comes suddenly, do not let him find you sleeping. What I say to you, I say to everyone: 'Watch!' "

Mark 13:32-37

Chapter 12

The Wisdom

of

Preparation

The word "watchman" evokes an image of the lonely sentinel who must keep guard during the dark hours when most others are asleep. The classical punishment for a sentinel who sleeps at his post is death.

Discovery Point:

My saving faith is always growing.

Several centuries ago a young soldier was doing sentry duty at the royal castle of Windsor in England. At some point between midnight and dawn in making his rounds, his commanding officer failed to see the young solider in the deep shadows of the castle walls and laid a charge against him for sleeping. The panel of officers were unimpressed with his claim to innocence and demanded proof that he had been awake. To their amazement the sentry said that he had heard the clock strike midnight, but instead of the usual twelve strokes, it had struck thirteen times! They didn't believe him, but further investigation found a number of other people who had also heard the clock strike thirteen times. It was a phenomenon that had never occurred before and has never happened again. The military court was forced to dismiss the charge. The young soldier's alertness in not only watching with his eyes but with his ears too had saved his life.

The importance of being watchful is a recurrent theme in both the Old and New Testaments. It is maintaining a state of readiness for any eventuality, expected or unexpected. Christians have a responsibility for maintaining a state of spiritual alertness on behalf not only of their own souls but also for the souls of others.

The Second Coming

The second coming of Christ and the final judgment of mankind is an event that evokes emotional extremes of all kinds. For one person, the emotion may be naked fear; for another, anxiety; for another, resignation, acceptance, desire, or any other emotion all the way through elation. The emotion is directly related to the person's relationship with God.

In truth, there is no reason for any emotion other than exhilaration and anticipation for a Christian who is preparing himself daily for the return of Christ. It will be a more joyous return by far than that of the prodigal son. And the celebration of the righteous will be a party like this earth has never seen.

Parable of the Ten Virgins Matthew 25:1-13

To illustrate how we should anticipate the Second Coming, Jesus tells a story. He begins this puzzling parable of judgment with the expressive "At that time . . . ," referring to the situation described at the close of chapter 24 (i.e., the unannounced coming of the master). This story is about ten young, unmarried women who make up a bridal party assembled to await the arrival of the bridegroom and his entourage. It is obvious from the context that the virgins represent the church, and the bridegroom is Christ himself. There is a temptation to identify the five who were foolish as nominal Christians and the five who were wise as true Christians. That does not, however, fit the virgin motif, which suggests that they were all pure (and therefore cleansed by the blood of Christ). In fact, they were just alike in many respects.

First, they were all invited to the wedding feast—none were "gate crashers."

Second, they had all accepted the invitation and were looking forward to the bridegroom's arrival.

They were also all alike in their knowledge and in their ignorance. All of them knew the bridegroom was coming, but none of them knew when.

All the virgins had lamps. They had the same potential opportunities.

All their lamps had some oil, because it is apparent from the statement in verse 8 that even the lamps of the foolish virgins burned momentarily.

All of the women became drowsy and fell asleep. If only the foolish virgins had fallen asleep, we could interpret the statement to mean spiritual sleep. But since the wise virgins also slept, it is obvious that physical death is meant.

And finally, even when the herald cries, "Here's the bridegroom! Come out to meet him!" they all still expected to attend the feast.

But then a critical difference between the foolish virgins and the wise virgins becomes evident. As they all adjust their lamps, the wicks of the wise virgins

burn brightly, but the lamps of the foolish ones
flicker and go out. A lamp can only burn brightly
when it has an adequate supply of oil. In the case of
the wise, they had prepared for a possible extended
wait before the wedding supper by carrying extra oil.
This possibility had apparently not occurred to their
foolish sisters, whose oil soon ran out.

A painful scene followed in which the five now
frantic unprepared virgins asked to borrow oil from
their wise friends. The wise virgins pointed out that
if they shared their oil they would soon be in the
same predicament. They suggested instead that the
foolish girls go to the merchants and buy oil. This
they tried to do, but it was too late. While they were
gone, the bridegroom arrived and took those who
were ready into the banquet room and closed the
door. When the unprepared virgins returned with
their lamps relit and requested admission, they were
refused because the bridegroom didn't know who
they were.

The Watch

Jesus ends the parable with a general warning:
"Therefore keep watch, because you do not know the
day or the hour." It is important that we understand,
as far as we can, the important elements of the
parable.

First, all the young women appear to have been
identical in the short term. If the bridegroom had
come earlier in the evening, they would all have
entered the banquet hall with brightly shining
lamps. But since he was much later than they had
expected, only five had enough fuel to be ready.
Jesus had warned in the preceding chapter that
many would not have the steadfastness to resist
worldly pressures and run the entire course: "Because of the increase of wickedness, the love of most

will grow cold, but he who stands firm to the end
will be saved" (Matthew 24:12, 13).

We have assumed that Jesus was talking about
Christians, and we may reasonably infer that the
lights (the radiance of the lamps, not the lamps
themselves) represent what is visible to observers.
Jesus had said earlier to his disciples, "Let your
light shine before men, that they may see your good
deeds and praise your Father in heaven" (Matthew
5:16). The world around us evaluates the genuine-
ness of Christianity based upon the good and positive things that Christians do and say, rather than
by their claim to have faith and be Christians. As
James said, "Show me your faith without deeds, and
I will show you my faith by what I do" (James
2:18b).

True, saving faith expresses itself through love

Second, the lamps are the tools or vehicles for
producing the light, and there is no indication in the
parable that there was any difference in the ten
virginal lamps. All the lamps were functional, if they
were properly fueled. They represent the individual
talents, gifts, and opportunities which God has given
his children to use in glorifying him.

It is the third element, the oil, that made all the
difference in the testing of the young women. The
wise virgins had plenty of oil to last for the entire
period until the bridegroom arrived; the foolish ones
did not. What can the oil possibly represent? It is
what makes the lamps give their light. So, if the
light represents Christian service, and the lamp
stands for talent or ability, then the fuel that ignites
the talent to produce works that glorify God must be

faith—not faith in the narrow sense of intellectual belief, but the commitment of one's whole being to the purposes of God. It is a faith that gives us victory over the world (1 John 5:4). Because the Thessalonians had preached the gospel throughout Macedonia and Achaia, their faith was known everywhere (1 Thessalonians 1:8). True, saving faith expresses itself through love (Galatians 5:6). And it is the only light for the world lost in darkness.

Assurance of Salvation

All ten of the young women in this story went to sleep (died) thinking they would awake in heaven (at the wedding feast). Five of them had obviously placed their confidence in the wrong thing and did not awake in heaven, but they awoke outside in darkness. The nagging question then is, "How can I know for sure that I am saved?" First John 5:13 says that these things have been written so that you may know that you have eternal life. It's not something you have to question, and it's not something for the future. You can know for certain that you already have eternal life with God. So, what did the five wise virgins know that the five foolish virgins did not know?

- Serving God well gives you great assurance (1 Timothy 3:13).

- Being confident and continuing to do God's will brings rich rewards (Hebrews 10:35, 36).

- Continuing in God's service gives you great confidence to face him on the day of his second coming (1 John 2:28, 29).

- Showing God's love to others in this life gives you great confidence on the day of judgment (1 John 4:16, 17).

All of these confidence statements seem to be tied to *doing* things for God. Should we infer then that our works (doing) earn us salvation? Paul struggled with this same question, as is shown in 1 Corinthians 9:27 where he "beat his body to make it his slave" for fear of "losing the prize" (salvation). And, yet, he concludes in Ephesians 2:8, 9 that salvation, from first to last, is available only by the grace of God through our faith in him. He is saying that he can tell by what he is doing and why he is doing it that his works are a *result* of his gratitude for having already been saved, not an effort to achieve salvation at some point in the future.

Paul knew that because his basic nature was now under the influence of the Holy Spirit, his new natural actions would be to do the things Christ himself did, out of the same motivation Christ had.

Good works are the natural expressions of saving faith.

He simply loved people with the love of God. Each of us who possesses this saving faith also has this new natural life style. "If anyone is in Christ, he is a new creation; the old has gone, the new has come!" (2 Corinthians 5:17). Since we Christians are being renewed each day into an ever clearer image of Christ, we will experience the same motivation Christ and Paul experience—service out of love and gratitude.

Doing spectacular things for God is obviously not the key to salvation, as Matthew 7:21-23 points out. Notice Jesus' response to those who said, "Lord, Lord, did we not prophesy in your name, and in your name drive out demons and perform many miracles?" He said, "I never knew you. Away from me, you evildoers!"

In contrast, the judgment scene shows those who are saved as the ones whose new natures are causing them to do all things in accordance with the nature of God—love for others without prejudice. That is what we are called to do as we wait for the return of the bridegroom.

There is no contradiction between Jesus' teaching in the parable of the ten virgins and Paul's statement in Ephesians 2:8, 9: "For it is by grace you have been saved, through faith—and this not from yourselves, it is the gift of God—not by works, so that no one can boast." Salvation is God's gift through Christ, which can in no way whatsoever be earned by good works. It is grasped by faith, a faith that works out of overwhelming gratitude and love for that salvation. Good works are the natural expressions of saving faith. If the lamp no longer gives its light, it's because there is no longer any oil. If the works cease, it's because the faith no longer exists.

If we give up and surrender again to the world, we will not be ready when the bridegroom comes. God says through Ezekiel, "If a righteous man turns from his righteousness . . . none of the righteous things he has done will be remembered" (Ezekiel 18:24).

Parable of the Watchful Servants Mark 13:32-37

As Jesus begins to relate this parable, he has just been pointing out some differences between the destruction of Jerusalem and his own second coming, which will be the prelude to the final judgment. Here are two important differences:

1. The destruction of Jerusalem would occur in that current generation, whereas there were no clues as to when Jesus would come again.

2. There were definite signs of the coming judgment upon Jerusalem. He compared these signs to a fig tree sprouting leaves as a herald of summer. But of *that* day or hour (the second coming) nobody, including himself and the angels, knew when it would occur. Only the Father knew. So, it is important to be ready all the time.

He compared his second coming to a house owner who went on a journey. Before he left, he assigned work for each of his servants to do during his absence, especially warning the doorkeeper to be on the alert.

Throughout the Christian age men have tried to find out the time of the Lord's coming at the end of the age. Many dates have been set for that earth-ending event, but the announced times have come and gone without anything unusual occurring.

"Therefore keep watch because you do not know when the owner of the house will come back—whether in the evening, or at midnight, or when the rooster crows, or at dawn." (verse 35). The time of Jesus' return leaves no room for religious opportunism because it is a secret of God that no man can find out. Paul wrote this in 1 Thessalonians 5:1-3: "Now, brothers, about times and dates we do not need to write to you, for you know very well that the day of the Lord will come like a thief in the night. While people are saying, 'Peace and safety,' destruction will come on them suddenly, as labor pains on a pregnant woman, and they will not escape."

What the Thessalonian church knew well has apparently escaped many self-proclaimed prophets since, because many dates have been published for the Lord's return, but he never kept any of them. One certainty exists, though: When the day *God* has chosen rolls around, the secret will be out, and "at the name of Jesus every knee should bow" (Philippians 2:10).

Jesus warns us to "watch," not in order to find any
signs of his coming, because there are none, but to
maintain a constant state of readiness so that it will
not matter when he comes. In any case, given man's
mortality and the fragileness of man's life, eternity
can come to any person at any moment via an auto-
mobile accident, a heart attack, or some other unpre-
dictable way.

In this parable Jesus tells us how to always be
ready. Each of us has been assigned a task, which
we are responsible for and which our Lord expects us
to faithfully fulfill. Do it! Work at your task with
your God-given gift every day, and you will be ready.

There is a danger here of our interpreting "assigned task" for works of merit, or earning our right
to eternal life. The parable is not focused upon
achievement or results. The point is commitment to
the maintenance of the Lord's household. No distinc-
tion is made between the relative importance of
assigned tasks or the differing productivity of individuals. It is a matter of running the entire course
and not giving up.

Only one responsibility is singled out for special
warning, that of the doorkeeper or watchman. A
watchman is not only responsible for himself but for
all those who depend upon him to warn them of
approaching danger (Ezekiel 33:7-9). The watchmen
of the Lord's household are the spiritual leaders
upon whom the Lord's people depend for guidance
(Hebrews 13:17), and the responsibility for guiding
others is not to be taken lightly for frivolous reasons
(James 3:1). At the same time, none of us can aban-
don responsibility for our own watchful readiness to
someone else. We must consider and evaluate the
guidance offered to us, for Jesus instructs us: "Consider carefully what you hear" (Mark 4:24), and we
must devote ourselves to faithful service to God

whether we receive encouragement and warning from others or not.

Expecting and Being Prepared

Expecting something and receiving it may be worlds apart. For instance, have you ever expected to receive something really special for your birthday only to be disappointed when something completely different was given? Your bubble of expectation pops and leaves you deflated, to say the least.

Or think of a little boy who has practiced hitting the ball all summer so he can make the Little League team. He gets chosen for the team, all right, but only as an alternate. And he ends up sitting on the bench all year. Can you picture his dejected face? But he doesn't quit practicing; he works out and hits the ball every day. Finally, in the last game of the season the coach sends him in because one of the other players got hurt, and he hits the game-winning home run. Exhilaration! Being prepared really paid off in the long run.

That's what being a Christian is all about—being prepared for the return of the Lord. If he weren't coming back, it wouldn't matter how we live. It wouldn't matter whether we were prepared or not. But his promises are sure, and he promised to come back and take us home with him. The bridegroom will be coming, and we must be waiting for him with our lamps full of the oil of faith and burning brightly for all the world to see. Then our expectations will be fulfilled, and even more than Cinderella with the prince, we will live happily eternally ever after.

Pearl of Wisdom:

*Faith that leads you to
salvation is an ever-
growing, ever-serving,
ever-loving faith, which
brings rich rewards and
joy.*

Focusing Your Faith

1. What emotions do you feel when you think about
    the Lord's coming again?

2. How do you personally keep from running out of
    oil in your spiritual lamp?

3. If you were the casting director for a movie being
    made based on the parable of the ten virgins,
    which of your friends would you cast as the
    bridegroom and which as prepared and unpre-
    pared virgins? Where would you cast yourself?

4. What at your church would change if every member were actively preparing for the Lord's return?

5. What does a true Christian look like to an unbeliever?

6. Why is the burning lamp in the parable of the virgins such a powerful concept? Why is it still timely today in an age of electric lights?

7. When the Lord returns, what sounds do you think will be heard on the earth?

Parable of the Wedding Feast

Jesus spoke to them again in parables, saying: "The kingdom of heaven is like a king who prepared a wedding banquet for his son. He sent his servants to those who had been invited to the banquet to tell them to come, but they refused to come.

"Then he sent some more servants and said, 'Tell those who have been invited that I have prepared my dinner: My oxen and fattened cattle have been butchered, and everything is ready. Come to the wedding banquet.'

"But they paid no attention and went off—one to his field, another to his business. The rest seized his servants, mistreated them and killed them. The king was enraged. He sent his army and destroyed those murderers and burned their city.

"Then he said to his servants, 'The wedding banquet is ready, but those I invited did not deserve to come. Go to the street corners and invite to the banquet anyone you find.' So the servants went out into the streets and gathered all the people they could find, both good and bad, and the wedding hall was filled with guests.

"But when the king came in to see the guests, he noticed a man there who was not wearing wedding clothes. 'Friend,' he asked, 'how did you get in here without wedding clothes?' The man was speechless.

"Then the king told the attendants, 'Tie him hand and foot, and throw him outside, into the darkness, where there will be weeping and gnashing of teeth.'

"For many are invited, but few are chosen."

Matthew 22:1-14

Chapter 13

You Are Invited

to the

Banquet

A̲t the end of World War II, the Russian head of state gave an elaborate banquet to honor visiting British prime minister, Winston Churchill. The Russians arrived in their best formal wear or military dress uniforms, but their honored guest did not. Churchill arrived wearing his famous zipper coveralls that he had worn during the German V-bomb attack in London. He thought it would provide a nostalgic touch the Russians would appreciate. They didn't. They were humiliated and insulted that their prominent guest of honor had not considered their banquet worthy of his best clothes.

Wearing the right clothing to a formal dinner honors the host and the occasion. Neglecting to wear it is an insult.

> **Discovery Point:**
>
> *I am clothed with Christ.*

The city police in Boston were reportedly the first local force to be put into special uniforms. The result was a dramatic improvement in their responsibility and efficiency. The officers tried to live up to the image created by their uniforms. Wearing the right clothes may not make the man, but they are likely to raise his level of confidence and performance, as well as the confidence and respect of others who see him.

Parable of the Wedding Feast Matthew 22:1-14

In the story of the improperly dressed wedding guest, Jesus teaches sensitivity to being properly clad for the occasion. Most people have had night-mares in which they were at an important social gathering where everybody else was dressed for the affair, but they themselves had forgotten to put on their shoes or had come in their gardening clothes.

The parable of the wedding feast is really two parables in one. Verses 1-10 tell about a wedding feast given by a king for his son. His invited guests spurn his invitation, which results in the king's armies destroying the city of those ingrates. The king then tells his servants to invite anyone who wants to come to attend the feast so his banquet hall is filled with guests before his son comes.

The second part of the parable in verses 11-14 describes an embarrassing moment at the banquet. The king notices that one of the guests is not wear-ing proper attire for the party. He asks why the guest has come without the right clothes, hoping to justify his behavior, but the man can offer no rea-sonable excuse. The king, therefore, orders that the man's hands and feet be tied and that he be thrown out into the night.

R.S.V.P.

Without doubt the king represents God and his son, Christ. The wedding feast (salvation) is timeless. It begins in earthly time and continues throughout eternity. It represents the joy and the countless blessings the redeemed enjoy in Christ's kingdom. The feast is beautifully described in Isaiah 25:6-9:

> On this mountain the Lord Almighty will prepare a feast of rich food for all peoples, a banquet of aged wine—the best of meats and the finest of wines. On this mountain he will destroy the shroud that enfolds all peoples, the sheet that covers all nations; he will swallow up death forever. The Sovereign Lord will wipe away the tears from all faces; he will remove the disgrace of his people from all the earth. The Lord has spoken. In that day they will say, "Surely this is our God; we trusted in him, and he saved us. This is the Lord, we trusted in him; let us rejoice and be glad in his salvation."

In the parable, the people for whom the supper was initially prepared were not thankful for the king's invitation to his table. This is a reference to the fact that God's covenant people, the Jews, would reject his gospel messengers who would bring them the invitation to eternal life. In this context it would suggest they rejected John the Baptist, the apostles, and all those who preached the Good News in the first generation of the church. In a broader sense they also rejected "all the prophets from Samuel on, as many as have spoken" (Acts 3:24).

But God's eternal purpose to save men through Christ into his kingdom is not frustrated by fickle mankind. When the Jews rejected God's invitation, they forfeited their right to preference, and the gospel was then preached to the Gentiles.

The king in the story was angry. The people who had known and enjoyed his blessings throughout their generations and were his special friends were the very ones who insulted and even killed his messengers. So, he destroyed both them and their city. This undoubtedly refers to the Jewish wars against the Romans in which there was a fearful toll of human life and extreme suffering. Jesus foretold the siege of Jerusalem by Titus and the horrors connected to it in Matthew 24:15-22. The temple was totally destroyed, and the Jews themselves, who had enjoyed much religious and political freedom before 70 A.D., were reduced to virtual slavery.

Jesus makes it clear in the parable that the Roman armies were acting for God by making the Jews pay for their ingratitude, for the abuse of their relationship to him, and for their cynical pretense of being God-fearing people. That does not imply, of course, that the Romans themselves had any righteous motives in slaughtering the Jews. God uses wicked men to work out his unswerving purpose for the world, even though those men are not aware of being used and would be unwilling to be used for such holy purposes if they knew it.

It must be pointed out that God in no way rejected the Jews as individuals or barred them from entering his kingdom (Romans 11:1, 2). But their rejection of Christ and the message of the apostles resulted in their losing the privilege of being in first place with God. In the early apostolic age, the gospel was offered first to the Jews and then to the Gentiles (Romans 1:16; Acts 13:46). Today the door into the kingdom remains open to "whoever wishes" (Revelation 22:17), whether or not he is descended from Abraham.

Never-Ending Party

The sequence of the supper continues in the parable, interrupted only by the arrival of the king himself. From God's viewpoint his kingdom is eternal. Its essential spiritual character flows without break from before the beginning of time through the present age and on through eternity. Those in Christ are alive already and will be forevermore (John 11:26).

From the human viewpoint, however, there are dramatic happenings within the scope of this parable. Jesus suddenly appears in the heavens, the universe passes away, and time ceases to be. The dead are raised, and the living are translated into a new dimension of existence (1 Corinthians 15:51-54). The judgment takes place, and the righteous are separated eternally from the wicked (Matthew 25:31-46). In God's mind real things are unaffected by the passing of temporary things (Hebrews 12:26-29). To God the kingdom continued without any disruption at all.

When the parable begins the king is obviously God the Father, but the king who arrives at the feast is just as surely Christ the King. He is no longer the suffering servant who hangs on the cross but the God of eternity (Revelation 1:8), now come to judge the world.

What Shall I Wear?

The first thing the king notices is that one guest at the feast has no right to be there. He has abused his host's hospitality by failing to wear the proper garments. Some scholars have understood this to refer to the caftan, or white robe, which in some Mideastern cultures was supplied by the host and given to each guest at the door by an attendant. This would mesh with other Scriptures referring to the garb of the saints (Revelation 3:4, 5, 18; 6:11; 7:9-13). Christ (that is, his righteousness) is the garment we are clothed with when we become Christians (Galatians 3:27).

This question naturally arises: How did the improperly clothed man get past the king's servants into the banquet hall? The answer seems obvious: They couldn't tell whether he had on the garment or not. Only the king could see that the man was a gate crasher. That implies that some people may be nominal Christians, members of the physical church but not members of Christ's true spiritual body.

God knows he did not give us the ability to see into each other's hearts.

And only God can know for sure. They may remain in the corporate fellowship until the King comes. Only he (or his angels) can sort out those who belong in the kingdom and those who don't (e.g., the parable of the weeds, Matthew 13:36-43; the parable of the net, Matthew 13:47-50). People are not competent to separate the saved from the unsaved. It's not our responsibility. In other words, we do not have the *ability* to respond to that task. It is beyond our ability. As 1 Samuel 16:7 notes, "Man looks at the outward appearance, but the Lord looks at the heart." That's not a condemnation of us. It's only an observation: God knows he did not give us the ability to see into each other's hearts. God reserved that response—ability—for himself.

What does that mean to us? It means that we can be fooled by what we see. Here are two ways we can be fooled:

- Some people, who don't exactly look right to us, are safe in the saving grace of God through their faith. We can't base fellowship on outward appearances!

- Some people, who look exactly right to us, are not truly part of God's church. We cannot avoid fellowship with them because we can't know who they are.

The offending guest of the parable fooled the king's servants. And he enjoyed the party for a short time. But, alas! He could not fool the king, who had him thrown into outer darkness where he would weep and gnash his teeth. Jesus ends the parable with a sobering statement: "For many are invited, but few are chosen." Is he referring to the "many invited" in verse 5 where his friends rejected his invitation? Or did he mean the ejection of the improperly dressed guest from the feast? Or did he mean both? Probably the latter. It is essential to understand that for our salvation we must accept his undeserved invitation. When we do, God is standing at the door of the kingdom, handing out our robes of righteousness that we must put on (Romans 6:1-18; 1 Corinthians 6:19, 20; Colossians 2:6-12).

Private Party?

It is possible, unfortunately, for one who has once put on the robe of Christ to take it back off. The point is, he must be wearing the robe—the only proper attire—when he comes into the banquet hall, or else he will not be allowed to stay.

The parable of the wedding feast does not suggest that God made a miscalculation by assuming that the Jews would gladly enter Christ's kingdom. Nor does it suggest that his original intent was to

restrict his kingdom to descendants of Abraham and
that inclusion of the Gentiles was a revision of his
original purpose that came about by the Jews'
refusal of his invitation. Such a false expectation on
God's part would deny his all-knowing nature. The
prophets clearly indicated exactly what would
happen in Isaiah 28:11, 12; 65:1-5 (compare to
Romans 9:27; 10:20, 21). Neither is the parable
intended to teach that no Jews would be present at
the wedding supper. It is not the purpose of the
parable to give specific information but to illustrate
general truths. Most Jews refused, and still refuse,
to accept Christ's invitation; they were rejected
because of unbelief. Yet, God remains willing and
eager to save them, as shown in Romans 11:1-6, 20-
24. In fact, the first church was entirely Jewish in
the beginning of the Christian faith, and the gospel
was preached entirely by Jewish tongues. That the
church was later made up largely of Gentiles was
not determined by divine decree but by human
choice. Everyone was ultimately welcome at the
feast.

Let the Party Begin!

A marriage supper in most cultures is a joyous
event. Not only the banquet itself but the occasion it
celebrates are high points in the lives of the guests.
There is a lifting of the spirit as the celebrants leave
their cares and worries behind and enjoy happy
fellowship and the joy of life. It is certainly significant that our relationship to each other and to God
in Christ's kingdom is so consistently represented in
terms of enjoyment.

Isaiah sings, "With joy you will draw water from
wells of salvation." Of those who pursue righteousness and who seek the Lord he says, "The Lord will
surely comfort Zion and will look with compassion

on all her ruins; he will make her deserts like Eden, her wastelands like the garden of the Lord. Joy and gladness will be found in her, thanksgiving and the sound of singing" (Isaiah 51:3). Joy in Christ is part of the fruit of the Spirit (Galatians 5:22).

A religious system that makes its followers fearful and unhappy is obviously not what God intended for his children. It is illogical that the God who let his only Son die to give us eternal happiness would design the resulting religion to make us miserable and insecure. Christians are to always rejoice in the Lord (Philippians 4:4); therefore it is appropriate that Jesus describes our walk with him as a joyous festival.

The salvation we experience through God's magnificent grace is to be full of joy, or it is not salvation at all. The source of that joy is the knowledge that we are properly clothed with the righteousness of Christ Jesus, and that we have been invited to the banquet. If our spiritual lives are not producing joy now in this life, this parable may well be saying we will not be in heaven to experience that joy either. You see, the party has already begun, right here on earth! The kingdom is now. The joy is now. The salvation is now. "Now is the day of salvation" (2 Corinthians 6:2). The grace of God is not something we work feverishly for all our lives and hope to get on the day of judgment. It is a reality today; all we have to do is reach out in faith and take it from the gentle hand of God who offers it to us in love.

Heaven on Earth

The church of Jesus Christ is intended to be a little bit of heaven on earth. It is an oasis from the world where we can find love and peace and incredible joy. It is an island where the shade trees are loaded with the delightful fruit of the Spirit and

where we can bask in the Son near the refreshing
water of life. In the church, by faith we feel the arms
of God hold us gently and protect us from the ever-
present dangers of the Evil One. In the church we
are safe (saved) from all harm. We are at home in
the palace of the King.

Our joy and gratitude overflow every time we
think of the King's grace and kindness toward us,
and we constantly try to think of things we can do
for him to say thank you. He has lavished wonderful
gifts on us. So, we find ways to use those gifts in his
service because we love him so much. And as a
result, our friends and family want to know him, too.
And his kingdom spreads.

Glory to God for his unspeakable gift of salvation!

Pearl of Wisdom:

There's a party going on! All I have to do is put on the right clothes, and I can go. The party is free, and the host is the King.

Focusing Your Faith

1. What is the proper attire Christians must wear to the party in the kingdom?

2. If the grace of God were a physical place you could visit, what would it look like?

3. Imagine that you are standing outside the door where God's great party is going on. What sounds do you hear?

4. If the *true* church is a little bit of heaven on earth, what will heaven itself really be like?

5. Why do you want to go to the banquet? Will your friends be going?

6. What are you using as daily reminders to be prepared for the banquet?

7. How can we ensure that we have an invitation to the eternal banquet of God? What can you do to help someone else receive an invitation?